Tell It Like It Is

A Resource
For Youth
In Treatment

By Alice Tallmadge
With Galyn Forster

SaferSocietyPress

PO BOX 340

BRANDON, VERMONT 05733-0340

Design & Typesetting: Sue Storey

Editor: Euan Bear

Printing: Quebecor Printing Dubuque

ISBN: 1-884444-46-6

Order from:

The Safer Society Press
P.O. Box 340
Brandon, VT 05733-0340

$15.00
Bulk discounts available

Acknowledgments

I would like to acknowledge and thank the following individuals (all of whom live and work in Oregon) without whose guidance this effort would not have been possible:

First and foremost, Galyn Forster, Looking Glass Counseling Center, Eugene; Dennis Bucklin, Hillcrest Training School, Keizer; Roxy Cooper, McLaren Training School, Woodburn; John Glassburner, Lane County Youth Services, Eugene; Pat O'Brien, Lane County Children's Services Division, Eugene; Peter Shannon, Sex Offender Counselor, Emerald Center for Behavioral Change, Eugene; Gerald Walters, teacher, Hamlin Middle School, Springfield; and Jesse Watson, Sexual Assessment, Trauma and Treatment, Salem.

I would also like to thank the many individuals who offered encouragement and support, or who took time to review the manuscript in the various stages of its evolution, including Bruce Janes, Steven Mussack, Gary Lowe, and Walter Bera. Your comments and suggestions were invaluable.

My heartfelt thanks to participants from McLaren Training School (Woodburn, OR), Looking Glass Counseling Center (Eugene, OR) and Emerald Center for Behavioral Change (Eugene, OR): Ben, Paul, Adam, Alexis, Yvonne, Eric, Monte, Steve, Barry, Kyle, Eli, Jay, Stace, Del, Mari, Karin, Shelby, Miguel, Jeff, Cal, Tom and the Masons. These people's willingness to share their experiences and learning with me make up the core of this book. Without them, this resource would not exist.

Publisher's Thanks

As always, we are indebted to our wise and experienced colleagues in the adolescent offender treatment field for their review and feedback. In particular, we offer our thanks to Walter Bera in Minnesota, Charlene Steen in California, Steven E. Mussack in Oregon, and Bruce Janes in Missouri for their careful reading and insightful comments. Without the generous contribution of time and expertise of these colleagues and many others, it would be much harder to carry out our mission of making available the best in treatment and training publications, helping offenders control their harmful behaviors, restoring victims, and making society safer for all of us.

About The Safer Society

The Safer Society Press is part of The Safer Foundation, Inc, a 501(c)3 private, nonprofit national agency dedicated to the prevention and treatment of sexual abuse. Founded in 1964 as the Prison Research Education Action Project by Quaker activist Fay Honey Knopp, the Safer Society Press published its first data on sex offender treatment in 1982. The Safer Society Press publishes an extensive collection of treatment-oriented books, audiocassettes, and videotapes for clinician training and victim and offender treatment. For a catalog, write to The Safer Society Press, PO Box 340, Brandon, VT 05733, call 802-247-3132, or visit our Website at www.safersociety.org.

Introduction for Treatment Providers

Tell It Like It Is is a resource to be used for adolescent offenders just entering or already involved in a treatment program. The book addresses major treatment issues using brief author commentary followed by quotes from offenders. The quotes — all from lengthy interviews — give the offender's perspectives or experience related to the issue being discussed, such as denial, lying, talking in group, identifying emotions.

Tell it Like It Is is directed primarily to offenders, but it will be very helpful for other interested parties — parents of offenders or victims, victims, teachers, school counselors, social workers, youth leaders, probation officers, etc. — who want to know more about sex offender behavior and treatment.

Meant to supplement existing treatment materials, **Tell It Like It Is** introduces critical treatment issues by letting young offenders speak directly to the reader. This approach, plus the book's simple writing style, is designed to make the material easily accessible to younger offenders.

While not specific to one particular treatment approach, **Tell It Like It Is** is based on a model that has as a primary treatment goal offenders accepting full responsibility for their behavior. This approach is taken from Anna Salters' Treating Child Sex Offenders and Victims, (Sage Publications, 1988) and is also the treatment model supported by the 1988 National Task Force on Juvenile Sex Offending (printed in the *Juvenile and Family Court Journal* Vol. 39, #2).

The handbook is deliberately organized to be flexible as to different providers' approaches and techniques. It begins with offenders' initial fears and anxieties about the treatment process, and proceeds to more complex issues. Since the chapters stand alone as to the issues they address, it is also possible to use chapters out of the order in which they are presented.

Although some adolescent sex offenders abuse people their own age, the majority are in treatment for abusing younger children. All of the offenders quoted in **Tell It Like It Is** abused children or younger people, and many of them had both male and female victims. The book approaches issues and chapter topics from this perspective.

Tell It Like It Is is not a comprehensive manual on sex offender treatment. For instance, the chapters on Thinking Errors and the Abuse Cycle only touch the surface of these very complex issues. Again, the purpose of this book is to use a peer-to-peer approach to introduce complex treatment issues, not to wrap them up in the space of a few pages.

Users may notice some repetition of material. Some issues dealt with in later sections shed light on issues covered in earlier chapters, and give those concepts additional weight and emphasis. Likewise, some phrases are introduced early on in the book, and developed in more depth in later chapters.

Each of the book's 13 sections is divided into short chapters. At the end of most chapters are questions that personalize the preceding material. These questions can be used in group or individual sessions to examine the target issue in more depth. The questions can also give individual offenders the chance to talk or think about their own experiences. When applicable, sections close with a list of important "Words to Remember."

The offenders' quotes in the different sections can be used to initiate discussions, to clarify particular issues, or to give a different perspective on how an offender has dealt with a particular problem. The chapters could also be used in group exercises with the group leader reading the introductory section, and group members reading different offenders' quotes. At no time should anyone infer that the offenders quoted are considered "cured" or "perfect role models." Some quotes lend themselves to further analysis for residual thinking errors, for example.

Tell It Like It Is also includes perspectives from female offenders, older offenders who have been through treatment, victims and parents. These are perspectives that may not be represented in group treatment or individual counseling, and can be used as stepping stones for further exploration and discussion.

None of the stories or individuals in this book are fictionalized in any way. All of those interviewed for this project agreed to participate because they whole-heartedly believe that treatment programs give adolescent sex offenders a chance — often their only chance — to learn, heal, and transform their lives.

Alice Tallmadge
Springfield, Oregon

Contents

Introduction

So, here you are in sex offender counseling or a treatment program. Some of you may have volunteered for treatment; most of you probably have no choice. Either way, what are you feeling right now?

Whether you are coming into treatment voluntarily or not, offenders just entering treatment experience a whole range of feelings.

For instance, some of you may be angry. You may feel you don't need to be in treatment. You may feel nervous, or even scared of what's going to happen next. Maybe you are going into group treatment, and are worried about what the other kids in the group will think about you. Most of you probably wish you could just forget the whole thing.

If you are having any of these feelings, welcome to the club! Your feelings are letting you know that you are starting something important. Sex offender treatment will give you a chance to look at yourself honestly, and to change some things about yourself you thought were impossible to change. Your treatment will give you a chance to increase your personal power. It will make it possible for you to have a life you never thought you could have, and for you to become someone you never thought you could be.

If you are reading this in a treatment program, you are a sex offender. A sex offender is someone who has sexual contact with another person that hurts that other person in some way. The hurt could be physical, mental, or emotional, or any combination. Usually, the person a sex offender hurts is younger or less powerful than the offender. A sex offender uses that difference in power to make the sexual event happen.

In this book, we use the words "offender" and "abuser" to mean a sex offender. We also use the words "offended" or "abused" to mean the same thing.

If you are in a sex offender treatment program, you have been charged with hurting others in a sexual way. You need treatment in order to understand and stop your sex offending behavior. The purpose of this book is to introduce you to some of the issues you'll be talking about in your treatment program.

About This Book

Tell It Like It Is uses a lot of quotes from interviews with teen sex offenders. The offenders talk about different parts of their treatment. They talk about how they felt when they first went into treatment. They talk about what was hard for them. They talk about what being in a group was like, and what they learned in their treatment.

The offenders in this book also talk about why they they began offending, and what they have learned to help them stop.

The offenders who talked with us for **Tell It Like It Is** are between the ages of 14 and 19. Most have between 4 and 9 victims; one has over 200. Most have victims of both sexes. Some of these offenders are in **lock-up** – that's a slang word for a juvenile detention facility. Others are in community treatment programs. That means they go to a treatment group or to counseling after school. Sometimes they talk about doing something "**on the outs**," which means in the world outside their treatment program or **lock-up**.

All of the offenders in this book agreed to participate because they wanted to help you out. They wanted you to know that they know that being in treatment isn't easy. It takes up a lot of time. It can be a big pain. They know that it can be scary or make you sad, or hurt, or make you really mad.

But they also know that treatment can help you overcome your fears and show you how to make positive changes. They know treatment can help you start being "real" with yourself and others. They know treatment can help you overcome your feelings of shame, and start feeling that you are a valuable person. They know treatment will help you build a good life and a good future.

How the Book Is Set Up

This book is divided into 13 sections. In the first 12 sections, each section is about one topic that you'll be talking about in your treatment. For example, there's a section on "Lying," one on "Feelings," one on "Your Family." These issues are complicated, so each section has a lot of different chapters. Each chapter talks about a different part of that issue.

At the beginning of each chapter, we talk about a few ideas and introduce some words that may be new to you. Then the offenders share their experiences and feelings about the idea we've introduced. They talk about how they acted when this issue came up in their treatment. They say if it was hard for them, and explain why. They say what they learned from it.

At the end of each chapter are questions for you to think about or to talk about with your counselor or group members. You may be asked to write some of the answers down.

Let's meet some of the offenders who'll be talking to you in this book. You'll notice they are different from each other. Sex offenders come from all walks of life. Anybody – a nerd, a doper, a jock, an honor student – can be a sex offender. It doesn't matter if you are rich or poor, or whether your parents are divorced, or even if you were a victim of abuse yourself.

Here we use the term **committing offense**. That is the crime the offender was charged with, that got him or her ordered into a sex offender treatment program. That does not mean that it's the only the offense that the offender committed. For example, someone who has offended against family members (incest) and others outside the family, but his committing offense is against a nonfamily member.

JAY is 16 and has been in a lock-up sex offender program for 9 months. Jay has had problems with drugs and alcohol. He began sexually abusing others when he was 11. His committing offense was Rape 1; his victim was his half-sister. (Having sex with a member of your family is called incest.) Jay has 6 victims.

ALEXIS is 15 and a sophomore in high school. She has been in a community treatment program for 7 months. Alexis offended her younger sister and brother, and she has two other younger victims. Alexis is the only female in her treatment group.

ERIC is 19. He has been in a lock-up treatment program for 9 months. This is his third sex offender treatment program. The other two were community programs. Eric started offending when he was 11. His committing offense was sexual assault. He has 34 victims, male and female. He has hundreds of offenses.

DEL is 16. This is his first time in sex offender treatment. He's been in a lock-up program for 4 months. Del comes from a very violent background. His committing offense was the rape of a younger boy. Del has 14 victims; one is his sister. He has both male and female victims.

STACE is 17 and a senior in high school. Stace molested a younger boy and turned herself in to the authorities. Stace was sexually abused by her mother for many years. Her mother didn't let her go to school. Stace was in treatment for 2 years. She says being in treatment "saved her life."

ELI is a smart 17-year-old with a "good guy" image. He's been in a community treatment program for 8 months. His committing offense was sexually abusing his two step-sisters. Eli started abusing when he was 10. His 4 victims were younger girls.

MONTE is 18. He loves music and is a jazz singer. He started offending when he was 9. Monte has been in a community treatment program for one year. His committing offense was molesting his two sisters. He has four female victims. Monte lives in a group home for sex offenders who are going through treatment.

BARRY is 18 and built like a football player. He has been in a lock-up treatment program for 8 months. In the past three years he has been in two other treatment programs. Barry started offending when he was 12; he has over 200 victims. Most of his victims were girls between 9 and 12 years old. His committing offense was offending a younger girl.

ADAM is 18 and an athlete. He's been in a lock-up program for 10 months. He began offending when he was 10. His committing offense was sexually abusing his sisters. Adam was physically and emotionally abused all through his childhood. Adam has 7 victims, all were younger girls.

YVONNE is 18. She first offended when she was 10, but stopped when she was 14. Yvonne was in treatment for two years. It was hard for her, because she didn't want to admit she was a female sex offender. Yvonne has gone back to school to get her GED.

BEN is 16. He is been in a lock-up program for 4 months; this is his second treatment program. Ben's committing offenses were 2nd degree sodomy with a younger boy and incest with his sister. Ben offended his sister over 300 times. Ben has 7 victims, male and female.

PAUL has been in an outpatient treatment program for one year. Paul offended his one female victim when he was drinking and doing drugs. He also had problems dealing with his anger, and says he used to be a bully to prove he had some power.

KYLE is 18 and has 7 victims. He says he offended partly to get attention from his mom, who was an alcoholic and "out at the bar every night." Kyle began offending when he was 9; his victims were all younger females and included family members. He was arrested at school.

O.K., now let's really get started.

Section 1.
Starting Treatment

Chapter 1:
What Will Other Kids Think About Me?

"I was afraid at first, because I knew what I did, but I didn't know if there was anybody else out there like I was."

Maybe you've spent many years thinking you were the only sex offender around. You hid your offenses and never talked about them to anybody.

Now, in sex offender treatment, people want you to talk about your offenses. That can feel strange and scary. It can feel like you are being asked to show secret parts of yourself to people you don't even know.

Some sex offenders cover up feeling afraid or insecure by putting on a really tough image. It may be the same "tough" image they use outside of their treatment program.

When you have a "tough" image it means you always act like you're on top of things. It means never showing you're afraid or sad. It can also mean being a bully.

Most offenders don't want to drop their image when they come into counseling. They don't want to show their true selves to the group or the counselor. You might be feeling that way, too.

There are many reasons why you might not want to drop your image. Maybe you're angry at having to be in a sex offender program. Maybe you're ashamed or embarrassed. You may be afraid the group will think you are "sick." You might think the group will laugh at you, or gang up on you, or reject you.

Many times people use one feeling to cover up another. You might be showing anger on the surface, but deep down, you might be feeling very insecure about the real person who's underneath your "image."

Here offenders talk about the different feelings they had when they first went into treatment:

JAY *"I didn't give a care, didn't want treatment, didn't care about nothin.' Everything was a game to me. If I talked, I said something dumb. But really, I was afraid of letting my real feelings come out, of showing the real me, instead of the phony me. I've been hurt all through out my life. I didn't want to show anybody my hurt."*

ADAM *"I was scared. All my life I've had this thing where I had to look good in front of everybody all the time. Having to tell the group all the disgusting things I did really hurt me. I didn't want to deal with what I did. I just wanted to forget it and go on with my life."*

DEL *"I felt angry. But really I was scared of what was going to happen if I told about my sister."*

MONTE *"I was scared of making a fool of myself, of not being able to fit in."*

KYLE *"I was afraid I'd get laughed at. Or that I would start crying and get laughed at for crying. I cry pretty easy."*

PAUL *"I was scared because I didn't think I could trust the group. I figured that if I told, they'd think low of me, and that they'd tell everybody they knew what I'd done."*

STACE *"I was angry about having to go to treatment. I didn't think I needed it. I didn't think I was a sex offender. I thought I did what I was raised up to do. That I didn't really hurt nobody."*

There's no one particular feeling that's "right" to have when you enter treatment. There's no one feeling that's "bad" to have, either. In fact, in the first few months you'll probably feel a lot of different feelings. The important thing is to let yourself, your counselor and your group know what those feelings are.

At the end of each chapter are questions to think about, talk about or even write down the answers for.
You may find it helpful to talk about some of your answers with your counselor or in your group.

Questions:

What are you feeling now? Are you angry, afraid, numb, confused, withdrawn?

Are you having different feelings from these or the ones these offenders talked about? What are they?

If you feel afraid, what are you afraid of?

If you're scared, can you admit that to your counselor or group leader?

If it's hard for you to admit you're scared, why is that?

If you are in a group:

Are you afraid the group will think you are "sick" if you admit you're a sex offender?

What do you think group members will think about you?

Words to Remember:

Lock-up

Committing offense

Incest

Image

Reject

Chapter 2:
Taking The First Step

"We've all done the same thing. It's just different people that we've hurt."

What each of the offenders in this book found out in treatment was that EVERYONE in sex offender treatment has problems. EVERY teen who has hurt someone in a sexual way has messed up other people's lives and their own life in a big way.

They also found out that treatment is the one place where you can talk about being an offender. Your counselor understands what you're talking about. Kids in group understand what you're talking about and how you're feeling. They're all in group for the same reason you are.

You can be open in treatment. You are not the first sex offender your counselor has worked with. Your counselor already knows a lot about teen sex offenders.

Some kids worry about their privacy, especially in groups.

Sex offender treatment groups have a rule about that. As Paul says, "Everything you say in the group, stays in the group." That's called group confidentiality. It means you never talk about group members or their offenses to anyone outside of your group. Many offenders feel a lot better once they know other group members won't talk about them behind their back.

Your group leader or counselor has rules he or she has to follow when it comes to confidentiality. In some states, counselors must report it to authorities if sex offenders they are treating disclose any additional offenses. In others, an offender won't be charged for disclosing more past offenses, but will be charged for disclosing offenses committed while in treatment.

Your group leader or counselor will be able to tell you what the rules are in your area. If you aren't sure, ask. Honesty and full disclosure are important parts of treatment. Your counselor knows this. He or she will help make full disclosure possible for you.

Here offenders tell about how their feelings about being in treatment changed.

DEL *"After a while I knew kids in my group wouldn't say anything about me outside the group. That made me feel more trusting."*

PAUL *"None of my fears about group ended up being true. They don't think low of you. Each of the kids in the group has done equal, less or more of the same thing. Everybody's equal in there. We've all committed the same crime."*

MONTE

"Our group is where you can talk your problems through with a bunch of friends. We have a really close bonding. We're all offenders working on what we need to get done. That is to heal ourselves and have our victims not feel responsible."

ERIC

"Group helps people. Just getting other people's feedback is really helpful. You can see that other people in the group have the same behaviors you do. When you see those behaviors in somebody else, they really click in."

PAUL

"Group helps me deal with the problems that I've got. If I didn't, they'd build up in me, and I'd probably end up hurting somebody again. My attitude toward group is changed from when I first went in. Now during the week I try doing the stuff they recommend to see what happens. Like thinking positive, or not being so down on myself. And it works. My brain is a lot clearer when I do that."

These offenders found out that, once they decided to participate, treatment worked for them. Instead of making them feel bad, treatment gave them support to figure out their problems. Offenders who were in groups found out they weren't alone. They discovered they could trust others in the group, and learn from them.

Questions:

What do you need to know from the group or your counselor to make you feel OK about your treatment?

Is confidentiality an issue for you? Have you talked about that with your counselor or group?

Have you ever had friends who supported you and wanted you to do the right thing? How did that feel?

How do you think the group or your counselor can do that for you?

Word to Remember:

Confidentiality

Chapter 3:
Denial

"Me? Have a problem?
No way!"

When some kids go into treatment, they say they don't need help. Or that, well, maybe they have a problem, but they don't need any help fixing it.

BEN *"I thought touching little kids was just something I did, that I was going to correct my mistakes after a while. I told the counselors, 'I ain't as sick as some of these people here.'"*

BARRY *"When I first went to treatment, I felt like I wasn't a victimizer, that I could handle myself and take care of my own problems."*

KYLE *"I thought the other kids in the group were weird. That I didn't have anything in common with them."*

Lots of times saying you "don't need help" is a way of pretending you don't have a problem. That's called **denial**. **Denial** is when you lie to yourself and others. **Denial** is when you don't want to face the truth about yourself or things that you've done. Lots of people use denial to keep from facing the truth about themselves. Sex offenders almost always have big problems with **denial**.

Here two offenders talk about denial. Can you tell whether either of them still has pro-blems facing the truth about himself or his behavior?

DEL *"I didn't want nothing of it – treatment, support. I didn't want to talk, didn't want any help. I knew I had a problem, but I kept saying I didn't."*

ERIC *"When I first went to treatment here, I had an image that what I did wasn't that bad. I listened to all these people talk about what they had done and I thought, 'You're sick. I'm not that bad.' I still haven't admitted I have a problem, totally. Part of me wants to say, 'You're an OK guy. You can live through this without really dealing with it.' But each day that thought goes away a little more."*

DEL *"Most sex offenders who come in here may say, 'I'm a sex offender,' but almost all of them say, 'I've only got one hands-on victim,' or 'I only did this or that.' They don't see that other things they did are victimization, too. They want to think their committing offense is the only one they have. They're just built in that wall of denial."*

You can see from what these two offenders say that they are no strangers to denial. Are you? Denial can be very subtle. It can show up in not wanting to think about your behavior. Or maybe you want to make that behavior seem less important or less hurtful than it was. Sometimes people who are in denial blame others for the same kind of behavior they don't want to see in themselves. Have you ever done that?

Questions:

Explain what "denial" means in your own words.

Have you seen anybody – friends, family members, enemies – "in denial?" What behavior were they denying? Why?

Do you know people who are hooked on drugs or alcohol, but insist they don't have a problem? Why is that denial?

Why do you think people deny their behavior?

Have you ever denied your behavior?

Have you denied that you're a sex offender? Why or why not?

Words to remember:

Denial

Victimizer

Victimization

Section 2.
Let's Talk About Lying

Chapter 4:
Why It's Hard
to Tell the Truth

" 'I only have two victims.

I swear it.' Right."

Many sex offenders lie a lot. They lie about how many victims they have. They lie about what they did to their victims, or how many times. They also lie about lots of other things.

Think about times when you have lied, and afterwards. It's hard keeping track of all those lies, isn't it? You have to always watch what you say, so you don't say much. A lot of times you have to pile new lies on top of the old ones. Lies are heavy, like stones. They weigh you down. They can make you confused about who you really are.

One of the biggest – and hardest – steps sex offenders take is deciding to tell the truth – about all their offenses and victims, about their true feelings, about everything.

But telling the truth isn't easy, is it?

Sometimes offenders don't tell the whole truth about their victims or offenses because they're afraid they'll get into even more trouble with the law. (If you don't know what will happen if you talk in treatment about offenses you haven't been charged for, ask your counselor, probation officer or group leader what the rules are.)

Telling the truth means admitting that you really are a sex offender. Telling the truth means facing that you have hurt people.

Telling the truth usually has **consequences**. **Consequences** are the things that happen as a result of something else happening. For instance, the **consequences** of telling about more victims or more offenses might be upsetting your family or making them angry or disappointed in you. It might mean you'll have to change your living situation.

Lying also has consequences. The **consequence** of not telling the truth is that treatment won't work for you. You won't get better. Period. If you don't tell the truth about your offenses, you will offend again, no matter how many times you tell yourself that you won't.

NONE of the offenders in this book was completely honest about their victims or offenses when they first went into treatment. It took some of them months to get honest. Some took over a year, even two years.

These offenders explain why it took them so long to be truthful. They may use some words that are new. One is **disclosure**. **Disclosure** is another word for telling the whole truth about your offending behavior.

Some of them will talk about a **polygraph** exam. A **polygraph** exam is another word for a lie detector test. People use **polygraphs** to try and see if someone is telling the truth. Polygraphs don't hurt. They measure things like your heart rate or changes in your skin when you are asked questions. Polygraphs aren't always perfect. They can't be used in court to establish guilt for new offenses. They are used in some treatment programs. They help some offenders to tell the truth.

BARRY *"The main thing I've had a problem with in treatment is getting truthful. Throughout my whole life, I've lied. And I lied to cover up for lies. I was always*

afraid that if I told the truth, I'd get in more trouble. That's why I kept a lot inside. I failed 8 polygraphs. Finally, everything came out, and I passed my 9th polygraph. So, from age 15 to 18, it's taken that long to get truthful with myself."

ERIC *in my last treatment program for only one offense. So, in my head, I thought I didn't have to admit to any of my other offenses."*

JAY *"I wasn't honest about my victims because I was scared my counselor would tell the authorities and I'd get into more trouble. I wanted to hold up the image that I only had one victim, that my offense wasn't really that bad, that I was better than everyone else. I tried to fake it, but it didn't work. I still was feeling shitty. My counselor knew what I was doing. He told me I wasn't going to get anywhere if I didn't get honest."*

DEL *"I knew my sister was one of my victims, but I didn't want to say anything. I didn't know if I'd get charged for it. I didn't know if my peers would go off and say something behind my back. I would kind of tell half of what I did, but not the rest of it. I didn't want my mom to find out, because I thought she would disown me.*

YVONNE *"For me, the hardest part of treatment was admitting what I had done. I had a huge block. For almost a year, we talked about my family, my other problems. I just beat around thE* *bush so I wouldn't have to talk about my offending."*

Lying is always a way to avoid taking responsibility for your thinking and/or your behavior. **Taking responsibility** means that you accept the consequences for your behavior. When you **take responsiblity** for sexually abusing someone, you don't blame someone else for your offense. You don't make excuses for offending. You don't pretend it wasn't really "that bad." You do whatever is necessary to make up for what you did.

If you are not honest with yourself, your counselor and your group, treatment won't work for you. If you aren't honest in treatment, you will offend again.

Questions:

Do you have offenses or victims you haven't told your counselor or group about?

If you have:

>**Are you afraid of what will happen to you if you tell the truth?**

>**Are you afraid of what your family will say?**

>**Are you afraid of disappointing or hurting your family or others more than you already have?**

>**Are you afraid of getting in more trouble?**

If you haven't been honest in your treatment, write down why you aren't telling the truth. You don't have to show it to anyone. Think about what you wrote. Then read the next section.

Words to Remember:

Consequence

Disclosure

Polygraph

Take responsibility

Chapter 5:
Why Offenders Decide to Get Honest

"It took me a year to tell about my last 3 victims. That set me back quite a ways."

Offenders decide to tell the truth for different reasons. Sometimes it's because of pressure from their treatment group or counselor. Sometimes it's because offenders decide they want to get better. Sometimes because they finally feel they can trust the group to support them.

Some of these offenders only got honest after they had failed one or more polygraph exams. Do you remember that word from the last section? Polygraphs are machines designed to tell if you are telling the truth by how your body reacts when you are asked certain questions.

MONTE *"I was scared to death to tell about two of my victims, because one of them was my foster sister. My foster parents had done a lot for me. I knew that when they found out what I had done they would* be furious. But I knew I'd never be able to have a clear conscience unless I told."

DEL *"It took about two months before I told the whole truth. I learned the group wouldn't say anything about me behind my back. The staff gave me a lot of support and encouragement."*

ALEXIS *"For me, I just had to get comfortable talking about my offenses at all. At first I'd just bring up little pieces; then, about one month ago, I told every offense I could remember. I knew I had to, so I just went and did it. I was really upset. I didn't even care what the group thought about me."*

ERIC *"I've been in three different treatment programs over the past six years. I've flunked a lot of polygraphs. I finally passed my last polygraph about 3 months ago. All that time I wasn't being honest, I saw myself as a big, cool, macho guy that could lift up the world. All I was was a liar."*

YVONNE *"Getting honest wasn't something I just went and did. My counselor helped a lot. In a way we eased into things; then she pushed me. I went through stages: I'd let her in, give her a glimpse of the truth, then I'd close the doors. If they were to make hills and valleys out of my treatment, they'd have a mountain the size of the deficit. I had that much struggle."*

BARRY

"One thing that helped me get honest was one kid I've really come to trust. He passed his polygraph and was rooting for me to pass mine. I had somebody behind me, somebody who cared about me."

You may be wondering how long treatment lasts. There's a lot to learn in treatment, so it won't be a matter of a couple of weeks, or even a couple of months. Many offender treatment programs last 18 months, or longer.

How long you stay in treatment will have a lot to do with how hard you work at being honest, and how well you participate in your program. Eric chose to waste a lot of his teen years in treatment programs where he wasn't being honest. What choice will you make?

Questions:

Have you told the truth about all your offenses and victims?

For those of you who haven't:

What is getting in the way of your being honest?

What do you think might happen if you were to tell the whole truth about your offenses and victims?

What could your counselor or group do or say that would help you be more truthful?

For those of you who have:

What made you decide to tell the truth? Was it wanting to get better? Trusting the group or your counselor? A friend who was supporting you? Pressure from the group?

How long did it take you?

What feelings did you have before? During? Afterward?

Chapter 6:
After It's All Out

"When I finally told, it was a relief, getting all that pressure off my shoulders."

No matter how many assignments you do, or how well you do them, your treatment will not work if you don't disclose all of your offenses. Truth is the HEART of your treatment. If you are not truthful, nothing anybody says or does will make you get better.

Think about when you are sick. You take antibiotics to kill all the bad bacteria in your body. If the drug killed only some of the bacteria, you'd just get sick again.

It's the same way with telling the truth. If you only tell part of the truth, you'll offend again. You will know that you got away with lying. Sooner or later, you will have another easy opportunity to abuse someone, and you'll tell yourself, "I got away with it before, I can get away with it again."

Telling the truth will help your victims. Disclosing the names of all your victims means they have a chance to get the treatment they need, too.

Telling the truth is the best thing you can do for yourself in treatment. It can change how you look, act and feel. It can be the thing that opens the door for you to get better, and to feel good about yourself.

DEL *"Before I told about my sister, I used to isolate, not participate at all. After I told I started talking in group. Now most group members feel I'm one of the most supportive guys in group.*

It felt good when I finally told the truth. I got a load off my back. My mom still doesn't know, but she will. She may not forgive me, but she won't disown me."

JAY *"When kids in group finally get honest, you can tell. They're nicer, they're more appropriate. They're not so immature. They seem happier. They're not always down in the dumps."*

KYLE *"All the time I wasn't being honest I was scared they'd find out, that I would slip and say something wrong. It would scare me half to death. I was always trying to keep everything in. That actually wears you down more than it helps you. Now I don't feel like an outsider anymore. And I get a lot out of group."*

ALEXIS *"After kids get completely honest, they act more grown up, because they feel better about themselves. That's the way it was with me. I felt a lot better about myself, and I was more open in group."*

BARRY

"When you finally tell the truth, it's like a big burden gets lifted off your shoulders. You don't have all that weight to carry around. You don't have to try and cover up each lie and secret that you have. One kid passed his polygraph the other day, and since he wasn't keeping in all his secrets, the acne on his face just cleared up."

Questions:

How does it feel to tell the truth after having lied for a long time?

Have there been times when you have kept the truth from someone you cared about? How did that feel?

Have you come out with the full truth about your offending behavior?

If you have, do you act differently now? How?

How does lying close you off from other people?

Chapter 7:
Why Sex Offenders Lie

"I think it's because they don't want to think that they're really bad people. They're trying to forget some of the things they've done."

The offenders in this book say there's lots of reasons why sex offenders don't tell the truth. Some lie because they're afraid they'll get into more trouble. Some lie because they don't want to have to admit they truly are sex offenders. Not **disclosing** the whole truth is the same as lying.

One thing is for certain: if you lie during treatment, chances are good you'll **re-offend.** You can re-offend a person who has been your victim before, or you can re-offend by hurting a new person. **Re-offending** a victim is just as bad a crime as the first offense was.

Ben and Jared both lied during their first treatment program, and both of them re-offended. Here Ben tells his story.

BEN *"In my last (outpatient) treatment program, I was honest about my offending behavior in the past, but I wasn't talking about my offending in the present. That's why I re-offended again.*

Now I'm dealing with all of it. I had to bring up some embarrassing issues. It was hard, but I felt better once they were off my chest.

Being locked up really helped me get honest. I don't want to keep on offending, but I know I will if I'm not honest."

Jared is 15. He was in treatment for over a year for molesting one of his sisters. He never **disclosed** his second victim, another sister. Recently, he **re-offended** her.

Now Jared is locked up in juvenile detention. He'll be there for a long time. This is what he thinks now that he's in lock-up.

JARED *"I think the reason treatment didn't work for me was because I was only working on half of my offending issues. It's like playing with half a football team, or half a deck of cards. You just don't have it all. It just doesn't work.*

When I was in the program and not being honest, I didn't think about it. I shut it out of my mind. When I re-offended, I felt really bad about it. I wanted to tell the group, but I thought they'd kick me out.

I think now if I was back in the group it would help me a lot more, because now everything is out. It would be a whole new thing."

Ben and Jared lied because they did not take their sexual offending behavior seriously They did not want to accept the fact that they were sex offenders.

Here are other reasons these young offenders give for why they aren't honest.

PAUL *"I've seen 5 or 6 new guys come into the group since I've been here. None of them have been honest right off. They don't want to think that they're bad people, that they've committed a bad crime. They'd rather forget."*

MONTE *"Some offenders say they aren't honest because they're afraid of hurting someone else by telling – like the victim's family, or their own family."*

BEN *"Offenders aren't honest when they come into treatment because they think their issues are sick, deviant, disgusting. They don't want to be looked on as bad or child molesters."*

YVONNE *"Offenders are gonna deny it, they don't want it to come out. They don't want to be seen as inferior. They don't want people to think of them as less. They don't want to be belittled. They know the public will say they can't be trusted, that they should never be around kids again."*

BARRY *"I've met over 60 different people in the programs I've been in. I can tell when other kids are lying, because I used to act the same way. I try to talk to 'em. I say, 'You're really trying to pull it over on us, and I know it.' And usually it comes out that they are."*

For some offenders, it may take flunking several **polygraph** exams before they get totally honest and make a full disclosure.

Questions:

Do you think Ben and Jared would have re-offended if they had told the truth in their treatment? Why or why not?

Why do you think sex offenders lie?

Did or do you lie about offending or other behaviors? If you do, why do you? What do you get from lying?

If you are in a group, can you tell when another group member is not telling the truth? How?

Words to remember:

Disclosing

Polygraph

Re-offend

Section 3.
How Group Treatment Works

Chapter 8:
What Happens in Group, Anyway?

"If I've got problems at home or at school, I bring them up in group. We get it all worked out."

In this chapter, we will look at how sex offender treatment works. Some of you may be seeing a sex offender counselor one-on-one, but most of you are probably in a treatment group, or will be in one soon.

Treatment groups are not all exactly the same. They can have different rules or a different way of operating. But the same kinds of things happen in most sex offender treatment groups.

If you're in a group you may have assignments to complete, such as writing the details of your committing offense, or an **autobiography**. An **autobiography** is the story of your life — as much of it as you can remember. You will probably be asked to write a history of your sexual behavior.

As you go further into treatment your assignments may get harder. You may have to figure out and write down the steps you took that led up to your offending. You may be asked to write a **clarification letter** to your victim(s). **A clarification letter** is a letter you write your victims in which you take all the responsibility for your offenses.

Other things happen in group, too. Offenders get help figuring out problems they have with their families or with other people. Sometimes they talk about things that have happened in their past.

BARRY
"We have assignments we have to write up, like an autobiography, a detailed offense, and our cycle. Then we read them to the group and they ask us questions, to make sure we've told the whole story.

We also talk about problems different people have, or things going on in the group. Sometimes we discuss fun things, or personal things that have happened to somebody in the group."

PAUL *"We talk about problems we've had during the week. We discuss what we're doing to graduate from the program. We say if we've done any illegal things, or something against the group rules. If we have, we get a task, like writing a paper on not smoking, something like that."*

MONTE *"We have assignments, and each week we present our homework to the group. They go over it, check for what should be there. Maybe a letter won't have any emotion in it, or maybe the person doesn't really take responsibility for the offense."*

KYLE *"If I've got problems at home or at school, I bring them up in group. We get it all worked out. A lot of times I go in there with a crappy attitude, and when I come out I'm in a good mood."*

BARRY *"In group, you see there's other people who have the same behaviors you do. When you see those in somebody else, they really click in. And just getting other people's feedback is really helpful."*

Did you notice a change in some of the attitudes from when these offenders first went into treatment? When Kyle started treatment, he was afraid he'd get laughed at. Barry says watching other kids in the group helps him learn about himself.

You may feel angry or resentful that you have to be in treatment. You may feel like sitting there and saying nothing. You may feel like your counselor or group demands too much work from you.

If you let it, treatment can be one of your best friends. Treatment won't reject you for telling the truth. Treatment can teach you tools to stop your offending behavior. Treatment can help you feel better about yourself and your life. But your program won't do that for you if you just sit there. You have to participate, and that means doing your assignments, speaking up in group or with your counselor, listening to other kids.

Questions:

What assignments have you had in your treatment program?

What did you learn from doing them?

Have you tried bringing problems before your group or counselor? If so, what happened?

How can your treatment group or your counselor help you?

Words to Remember:

Autobiography

Clarification letter

Chapter 9:
Listening Helps!

"When they say what they've done, I think through what I did."

A lot of these offenders say it helped them to listen to other kids tell about their offenses. Here they explain why.

ADAM *"When they say what they have done, I think through what I did. I get a learning experience. Plus, I knew how to help them out when they needed it, and that makes me feel good."*

STACE *"Group was good because I knew I wasn't the only one who had done this. I wasn't the only one suffering. A lot of them had hurt pasts, too."*

ERIC *"I'll be listening, and inside I'll be saying, 'They can admit it. They can say it. I wonder if they're feeling all confused and mixed up like I feel when I talk about it?' You just need to get it through your head that that you're no different from these guys. They've heard it all before."*

ALEXIS *"When other people are talking about their offense, it makes me feel better, sometimes, knowing I wasn't the only one who did this certain thing. It makes me feel a little bit better."*

PAUL *"Sometimes it's weird. Listening to other offenders makes being in group easier, because I know we've all done something similar."*

For some, listening to others in the group helps them feel less alone. Others say it gives them courage to speak up about offenses or thoughts they haven't disclosed yet. That's called **support. Support** is when someone is on your side in a healthy way. If you let it, the group can support you and give you courage to say what you need to say.

On the other hand, sometimes the group can challenge you, too, or make you feel uncomfortable. Read about that in the next section.

Questions:

Does it help you to hear about other offenders' behavior? How?

Does it make you feel less alone when you hear other offenders talk about their behavior?

Does listening to other offenders help you see your abusive behavior in a different way? How?

What does it feel like when someone really listens to what you are saying?

Word To Remember:

Support

Chapter 10:
Sitting in the "Hot Seat"

"I felt embarrassed, but I knew I had to talk about my offenses. I felt shame, disgust."

One of the hardest parts about group is telling about your offenses. It's an important part of group. When you talk out loud about your offenses, they become more real to you. You can start to see yourself and your behavior in a different way.

Here the offenders talk about how it feels to get up in front of the group and talk about their offending behavior:

ELI *"It's embarrassing. And it's shameful. It was really difficult at first, harder than I thought it would be."*

JAY *"I was embarrassed, because when I first got there I said I only had one victim, but I have 5. I tried to make what I did real minimal, so I'd think I was better than everyone. I just didn't like people talkin' about it. It's hard."*

BEN *"I was embarrassed to say what I had done. I didn't want the group to think of me as really sick.*

But I knew I had to. I felt shame. Disgust. I wasn't feeling disgust before I said what I did, but after I did. That helped me a lot, to see how disgusting my offenses were."

ERIC *"My stomach gets all knotty. I have to let the group know what kind of person I am, and I don't like doing that."*

STACE *"It was hard. 'Cause there was a lot of guys in group, and I had sex offended a boy. It was kinda hard to talk about it with guys there."*

ELI *"It was like letting out a dark secret that you didn't want anybody to know about."*

MONTE *"Everybody hates it. No one likes telling their story, no matter how many times they've done it. I've probably gone over my offending history 20, 30 times in group. Each time it gets a little easier, but I never like talking about it."*

ALEXIS *"If I'm talking about my offenses, and it's something new that I didn't bring up before, I'm scared of what the group is going to say, or how they're going to act. I don't get as scared as I did the first time."*

BARRY *"It was scary, because I have more victims than anyone else in my group. Now every time I go through and think about the people I victimized, I get sick to* *my stomach. It just makes me sick to think of all those people that I hurt."*

Not only do you have to talk about your offending behavior in group, but often you have to listen to what other group members have to say about it. This is important. Others in the group can help you see where you aren't thinking clearly. They can point out if you are making excuses for your behavior, or blaming somebody else for things you've said or done.

Sometimes, what other kids say can really make you mad. Sometimes kids don't want to hear what you have to say, either. That can make you mad, too.

You may feel **aroused** when you talk about your offending behavior or when you hear other offenders talk about theirs. **Arousal** is when your body reacts to sexual information. If this happens to you, don't feel ashamed about it. It's normal to feel aroused when you hear sexual information. Treatment will help you learn to control your sexual arousal to appropriate situations. It will help if you talk about this with your counselor or in your group.

These offenders had to struggle with talking about their offending behavior in group, but now they say it's helpful.

ALEXIS *"Sometimes when the leader has the video camera on me, it feels like the group is trying to get everything out of me. It kinda feels like they're ganging up on me."*

PAUL *"When people first made comments it made me mad. After a while I figured out that's what they're supposed to do. I still get mad, but I've also become more honest."*

STACE *"Sometimes they'd call me on stuff, like if I made an excuse. Mostly they were really helpful."*

ELI *"When they ask me questions, they make me reveal things I didn't plan on telling. That made it real hard, too."*

ERIC *"Being confronted made me really angry. I felt the group was out to get me. I was the new kid and they wanted to see how far they could push me.*

Inside I'd think, 'I can fake it through this. I don't have to listen to what you guys have to say. I'm not that bad.' After a while I realized I was wrong, that the group did want to help."

DEL *"If people in group made real negative comments about things I said, I would get real intimidating towards them. Or I would take a victim's stance. I would make it look like they were the bad guy. A lot of sex offenders use that – playing the victim."*

A treatment group and/or your counselor can be like a mirror. You may not want to hear what they have to say about you, but you can bet they are showing you who you really are.

That's hard, but it's also how people grow up. How can you fix something if you don't admit it needs fixing? Your group or your counselor will let you know which of your thinking and behavior patterns need fixing. They will support you if you are willing to change.

Remember, everybody in your group is a sex offender. You are all in the same boat. They don't want to hurt you, but they don't want you to slide by, either. They want to help you change your life – and they want you to help them change theirs.

Questions:

How do you feel when you talk about your offending behavior?

Does talking about your offenses make you see them differently? How?

Does it make you mad when other kids ask you questions, or don't believe you or challenge you? If so, what do you do when that happens?

Do you get aroused talking about your offenses or hearing about offending behavior? Is it a problem for you? How do you handle that?

If you've talked about your offenses in group, what kind of responses helped you? What kinds of responses weren't helpful?

> ### Word to Remember:
>
> **Arousal**

Here we are, talking about what goes on in treatment. And you're finding out that treatment isn't just about sexual offending. It's about a lot of things. It's about why it's important to tell the truth – about your offending, and in all the other parts of your life, too. It's about learning to accept the **consequences** of your behavior. It's about learning from others, and helping others learn about themselves.

In treatment, you learn what it feels like to **take responsibility** for your offenses in front of your counselor or the group. You learn how to confront someone in a helpful way when they're not being honest. You learn that lying hurts yourself more than anybody else. You learn how to help youself and how to help other people, too.

In treatment you get a chance to learn about and understand your feelings and attitudes. You see how you act when you're confronted by your peers. You see what you like about yourself, and what you don't. You can discover who you really are behind your "**image**."

No wonder sex offender treatment takes months to complete. No wonder it can feel so confusing. It's all about learning how your attitude, feelings and behavior are connected. It's learning that changing your attitude can truly change your behavior. In many ways, sex offender treatment is all about growing up.

Section 4. Feelings

Chapter 11: Why We Talk About Feelings

"Feelings are a problem for me because I have too many. They're all crumpled up inside my head."

You didn't just wake up one day and discover you were a sex offender. Offending is the result of a long line of negative thoughts, feelings and behaviors that build up over time. These feelings, thoughts and behaviors are the stairway that leads to your offending.

Feelings play a huge part in all our behaviors, including sexually offending behavior. Feelings are a big problem for sex offenders. A lot of sex offenders **stuff** their feelings. That means they bury them. They might let themselves feel good or angry, but between those two feelings is a big black hole. They don't admit to ever feeling sad, ashamed, confused, frustrated, depressed or hurt.

Offenders stuff their feelings for different reasons. Sometimes it's because of abuse from their past. Some offenders grow up getting the message that the only OK emotions are happy, angry or horny. Others are taught it's bad or "wimpy" to admit to feeling sad, lonely or depressed, even though those feelings are natural and normal.

The reason many offenders can abuse others is because they stuff most of their feelings. If they feel hurt or sadness or low self-worth, they stuff it. They tell themselves those feelings don't count. After a while, they act as if other people's feelings don't count, either.

For instance, take an offender who doesn't admit feeling sad about the times he was hurt by people he trusted. He might work to get younger kids to trust him. Then he intimidates or even offends them. Because he can't (or won't) feel his own hurt, he can't admit that he's hurt his victims.

What that offender did was to **get back**. A lot of teen offenders do that. Some hold in their anger until they finally explode. When somebody hurts them, other offenders get back by hurting somebody else. **Getting back** can include bullying or intimidating someone. It can mean sexually abusing someone, too.

A big part of sex offender treatment is learning to "unstuff" your feelings. You learn to identify what you are feeling. You learn it's OK to feel bad, insecure or scared. You learn that not admitting those feelings can make it harder to feel positive feelings, like satisfaction or happiness.

You will also learn how to express your feelings in healthy, non-hurtful ways. You will learn to tell people what you are feeling and what you need from them. You may find you can express your feelings by drawing, playing music, writing, acting in plays or building something. You might find that you can use games or sports to release certain feelings.

You'll discover that the more you express your feelings in healthy ways, the less you'll feel the need to "get back."

Learning about your feelings is a big key to learning about and liking who you really are. When you express your feelings, you discover who you really are behind your **image**. You let others see who you really are, too. This is scary, at first. Then it's a big relief.

If you don't learn to identify and take care of your feelings, you will end up feeling like you don't have any power in your life, or that your self isn't worth much. You might already know what that feels like.

ELI *"It's not that I didn't have feelings before I went through treatment. I had all the feelings I enjoyed. But anything that didn't feel good I completely wiped away. I wouldn't let myself feel it or talk about it.*

When you express how you really feel about a certain thing, your feelings start coming back. What also helps is the group asking me questions, forcing me to say what I feel."

JAY *"The hardest part of treatment for me has been figuring out my feelings. Feelings are a problem for me because I have too many. I feel this one second, this the next. But before I came into group the only feelings I would admit to were happy, sad and inbetween."*

DEL *"I used to think it was wimpy to cry, or be scared or anything like that. Now I know that's a crock. You're more of a man when you share your feelings."*

BEN *"I stuff all my feelings. Some was because my dad emotionally neglected me, called me names. I started shutting off my feelings from that. It was an escape.*

I've been in treatment for a year, and I'm just starting to talk about my feelings. I'm still confused, about my parent's divorce, stuff like that. I don't really like to talk about my mom and dad. That's why I shut off my feelings. I really don't want to break down and cry about it."

STACE *"The only feelings that I knew were happy ones. I didn't know sad, I didn't know angry. I knew depressed, but I didn't really acknowledge it. For awhile, I thought, if I can't feel, I guess no one else can feel either. I used that to get by."*

ADAM *"Before treatment, the only feelings I could express were my anger and the love I had for a few people. I couldn't cry or express when I felt rejected or betrayed. Here I've had to go back and relive all those feelings. I had a lot of abuse in my life, and I had to relive a lot of hard feelings.*

Now I know what rejection feels like, what all those emotions feel like. And I'm not alone. I have people with me who know how to help me out. Back then, when I was a kid, there was no one there for me at all."

BARRY *"I've learned what different emotions are, and how it feels when they're inside my body. I can talk about them and get them out so it doesn't have to build up."*

Feelings make our lives rich and full. If you cut off the feelings that don't feel good, you also cut off many of the ones that feel great.

A really good feeling – like excitement or anticipation – can pick you up and give you a lot of energy. Low feelings teach you about the difficult parts of life. You don't grow up if you don't learn to deal with the hard times and bad feelings all people have to go through. Letting yourself feel those feelings helps you understand other people better. They can also inspire you to create something. Ever heard of a music style called "the blues?" Guess where that came from.

Learning about your feelings will also make you feel more powerful. Your feelings are always influencing you, whether you pay attention to them or not. Learning to identify and handle your feelings will give you more control over yourself and your behavior. We'll talk more about that in the next few chapters.

???▶

Questions:

Can you identify the feelings that you have, or are they a confused lump inside you?

What feelings are hard for you to deal with?

What feelings do you feel comfortable expressing?

Do you use your "image" to cover up certain kinds of feelings? If so, which ones do you cover up?

Can you tell someone to leave you alone without yelling at them? Can you tell someone you're angry at them without hitting them?

What does it feel like to not have any power in your life?

What feelings would you like to feel less of?

What feelings would you like to feel more of?

Words to Remember:

Stuff or Unstuff your feelings

Get back

Image

Chapter 12:
The Big Red A – Anger

"My anger's my biggest problem. It's one of the hardest things I have to control."

Maybe you've noticed that a lot of offenders talk about feeling angry. Anger is a very powerful emotion. Almost everyone has a hard time learning how to deal with anger in a healthy way.

Some people have a short fuse. They get mad fast, make a fuss, then settle down. Usually you know when these people are angry.

Other people bury their anger. Buried anger doesn't stay buried, it just pops up somewhere else. Sometimes buried anger explodes. Sometimes buried anger leads to reckless and hurtful behaviors, like bullying other kids, wrecking things or drinking a lot of alcohol at one time. Buried anger can also lead to sexually offending.

Part of sex offender treatment is learning to accept and handle all the feelings you have, including anger. You may talk about your anger in group, or maybe you'll get angry at someone in your group. Then you will have a chance to try new ways of dealing with your anger.

In the following quotes, offenders share their experiences with anger. They may use words that are new to you. One of them talks about **passive/aggressive** behavior. Do you know what that is?

Passive/agressive behavior is an indirect way of expressing anger. Lots of people, not just offenders, express their anger this way. Here's an example of **passive/aggressive** behavior: You're angry at someone, but you don't tell them. Instead, you might borrow something of theirs and break it. Or maybe you'll say something mean about them behind their back.

Usually people act in a **passive/aggressive** way when they don't know how to express their anger directly. Or when they don't feel they have enough power or are afraid to express their anger directly.

Another word used here is **appropriately**. It means to react in a way that fits the situation, doesn't hurt anybody and respects everyone involved. **Appropriate** ways of expressing anger include talking about your anger to a supportive person, going for a jog or giving your all in a basketball game. **Inappropriate** ways of expressing anger are yelling at someone, throwing a tantrum, hitting or breaking things.

Paul talks about using **closed channels**. **Closed channels** are when you shut everybody else out and refuse to hear what they are telling you, even if it is helpful. You may have used closed channels in group, with your counselor or with your parents or teachers.

JAY *"When I got angry on the outs, I'd hit things, throw things or walk off. I never fought in my life, never hit my victims, either.*

Here, when I get mad I usually talk it out with the person who confronted me. I tell him how I feel about what he did. If the person will talk with me, it usually works. If they won't, I talk to someone else. That can work, too."

DEL *"Sometimes in group if someone wasn't accepting what I said, I would get mad. My anger would short out really fast and I start talking really loud.*

Then I took a look at myself. I asked, 'How would I want the staff and peers to talk to me about this?' So, instead of yelling, I started talking to the person, as if everyone else in the group isn't there. And I usually get through, believe it or not."

BEN *"On the outs, I might tell people to f-off. Or do something slow, or victimize 'em. Now, I go to peer group members and tell 'em I was pissed off how the group went. Sometimes I'd rather hit 'em, but I talk to them instead. That's part of treatment, learning how to deal with anger appropriately."*

ALEXIS *"When I got angry in group I wouldn't show it. I'd just have a smile on my face and try to hide it."*

ERIC *"I never expressed my anger appropriately. I played passive/aggressive games. In here I hold my anger down, because I don't know how to express it. Or I do know, but I choose not to."* (Shortly after Eric said this, he assaulted another group member.)

ADAM *"I've been in fights all my life. When I got angry I would blow up. I've even hurt little kids. When I first came to group I'd get angry, but I kept to myself.*

Now when I'm mad I talk to whoever made me mad, or I talk one-on-one with one of my peers. Afterwards I'll go talk to the person I'm mad at. That way I don't blow up or do something I'm going to regret later."

PAUL *"When people in group prove me wrong, that makes me mad. I express it by being smart aleck and using closed channels. **Closed channels** is when I close everybody off and ignore what they say.*

Before when I got mad I would go around punching things, like walls and doors and people. Now I lie down and listen to the radio, or take a little jog."

STACE *"When I got mad or upset, I just carved on myself. I had to learn that I didn't have to hurt myself everytime I got angry or sad.*

Now I know it's OK to be angry. When I was growing up, if I got angry, I got hit. If I backtalked I got hit. It's not right to backtalk, but it's normal, it's OK. Everyone gets angry. It's healthy and normal."

MONTE *"I always hid my anger.*
Always. It was the one thing I never really showed. Only time it ever showed was when I hit my sisters, or let it build up so much it would just explode.

Now, in group, we talk about it when we're angry. We say, 'I'm angry. Here's why.' You work through it. You talk about it. I think that's one of the biggest things I've learned."

Did any of what these offenders said sound familiar to you? There are many different ways of expressing anger. Anger can give you a lot of energy. If you focus your anger into something like chopping wood or whacking weeds or cleaning your room, it can help you get a lot done.

You also need to learn to switch your focus from what made you angry to what you can do to make things go better for you.

Sometimes you can't go back and talk to the person who made you angry. If you can, it's a good idea to do that, after you've cooled down. In group or in your counseling you can practice ways to talk to someone who has made you angry. You can practice talking about your anger without acting it out.

Questions:

How does your body feel when you get angry?

When you are angry, do you stuff it or do you express it? How do you act?

What are some inappropriate ways to express anger?

How do you express anger appropriately?

Give an example of passive/aggressive behavior. In what ways do you show passive/aggressive behavior?

What part do you think anger played in your offending behavior?

Words to Remember:

Appropriate

Inappropriate

Passive-aggressive

Closed channels

Chapter 13:
Power and Control

"The biggest thing in my offending was that I wanted the power and control."

Power is something everyone has to learn to deal with. Almost everybody wants to live with a sense of power. If you don't feel like you have power in your life, you feel weak and vulnerable.

Power usually means being in control, having things go the way you want them to. You can have power over yourself, over other people, even over a game. People who have achieved a high level of skill in a sport, a game or in a profession have a lot of power in that area.

There are both negative and positive ways to achieve a sense of power. **Positive power** is having control over yourself, over others or over some area of life in a healthy way. Many teachers, parents or coaches are examples of people who have positive power over others. They use their power to help other people grow and feel good about themselves.

When you've accomplished something difficult you get a feeling of **positive power** because you have control over yourself. This could be when your team wins in sports, when you figure out a tough math problem or when you successfully fight an addiction to drugs, alcohol or sex.

Negative power is when you get your power by taking other people's power away. You might do this by using force, intimidation, threats or bribes. You are using **negative power** when you bully other people, or use your size or voice to scare smaller kids or peers into doing what you want them to. You use negative power when you manipulate people or lie to them.

Negative power and **positive power** can both feel good, but in very different ways. When you use negative power, part of you feels like you're "somebody." But deep down inside you may feel small. You know you've used power in a negative way. You may begin to use negative power more and more to cover up for feeling small inside. Some people get addicted to negative power.

When you use your power in a positive way, you feel good all the way through to your bones. You feel big inside. You don't need to take other people's power away because you can feel your own power inside of you.

Sex offenders use negative power. They get feelings of power from abusing others. Many offenders never learned ways to get positive power. Some believe they can't get feelings of power in positive ways. That's because they have **low self-esteem**. When you have low self-esteem – or lack confidence – you don't think you are worth very much as a person.

YVONNE *"Offending was like a power game. It was all about who's got control, about who can do what to the other person.*

When you offend, you get a rush – you get power. But then what happens is you get more hungry. You have to go back for more. It's like an addiction. You want more."

ADAM *"I was 9 or 10 when I first offended. I was feeling bad about myself, so I went out and got power from somebody else, and made them feel really bad. I thought it would bring me up higher, but it brought me down even lower."*

ALEXIS *"When I was offending my victims, I would make them have eye contact with me. That was how I knew they were paying attention to me. It made me feel that I had all the power, that I was in control of the situation."*

BEN *"I used to offend to get power. I didn't think I could get power any other way. All my life I've been told I was stupid and clumsy, so I didn't think I could have any power the way other kids got it. I was always told I was bad at sports, and I was. Now I've been practicing and I'm a lot better."*

DEL *"In group, when someone brought up an issue that showed the true me, the inner me, I'd make up negative things about them to make them look bad. Or I would walk out of group so I could take their power away from them. I'd do anything to get me back the power and control I wanted."*

In treatment, you will learn to tell the difference between positive and negative power. You will learn how your desire to feel power contributed to your offending behavior. You will also learn positive ways of achieving a sense of power.

Questions:

Have you used your power in a negative way to control other people? If so, how did that feel to you?

How else have you seen people use their power in negative ways?

Has anyone ever used negative power to get control over you? How did that feel?

How has wanting to have a feeling of power played a part in your offending behavior?

Words to Remember:

Negative power

Positive power

Low self-esteem

Chapter 14: Positive Power

"Positive power is accomplishing something. Doing treatment. People building you up. That's a good rush."

The offenders in this book have learned different ways to get positive power. Some feel power when they play sports or win at games. Others feel powerful when they express themselves by writing songs or poems.

PAUL *"I do something constructive, like baseball, volleyball, pool. Or I can go on a computer and play games that I'm good at. Before, I would push people around. I was like a big bully, picking on younger and smaller people."*

ADAM *"To get positive power, I do something I'm good at, like sports. Or sometimes by drawing, or writing songs and poems. Other people have read my poems and songs and liked them.*

Sometimes I get power by helping people. I helped this one guy. He didn't need to say thank you or anything. I could see it on his face. It's a way I can have power and feel good about it."

ELI *"When you express your feelings, you feel like you've gained some control and power. If you feel that things are completely out of your control, but don't say anything, nothing changes."*

YVONNE *"I get positive power now by standing up for myself. If there's a challenge, I fight for what I want. I toughen up. I struggle. If everybody says it's impossible, I do it anyway, like getting an A in a class. I don't just sit and say, 'I'll never be able to do this.' I used to. Not now."*

DEL *"Sports is one way. And school. I'm only 16, and I take college classes. I don't look at it as power, I look at it as control – that I'm taking care of business."*

ERIC *"Knowing I'm doing something that I'm good at, wrestling or playing basketball. Mentally I get a lot of power doing math, because I'm really good at it. But I have to be really careful. I can turn that around and use it as part of my image: 'I'm better than you are.'"*

STACE *"I like artsy-crafty kinds of things. It sounds kind of stupid, but when I'm making something I'm in control. It's something I can do, that only I am in control of."*

BARRY *"I used to be a couch potato* and not do anything. Now I try to play some sports. I'm big, but when I can beat one of the smaller guys here in a foot race, that gives me power."*

MONTE *"I love to sing. I'm in two* music classes at school. My vocal jazz class starts at 7:15 a.m. When I go in there, I may be dead tired. But if we sound good, I just get this rush. It can set my mood for the entire day."*

KYLE *"Driving my car. I ask my dad, then I drive* right up here on top of this hill and sit on the hood of my car. It's my thinking spot. It's like my third home."*

Questions:

What in your life gives you a feeling of positive power? Make a list.

How does having positive power feel different from having negative power?

Section 5.
Thinking Errors — Tickets to Offending

Chapter 15:
What Are Thinking Errors?

"People don't realize it, but everybody uses thinking errors some time or another. It's just criminals, like us, we use 'em to manipulate people, to get our needs met."

Maybe you've never heard the phrase **"thinking errors"** until just now. In treatment you're going to learn a lot about **thinking errors**. Sometimes they are called "cognitive distortions" or "criminal thinking."

Just what are **thinking errors**?

Thinking errors are twisted thinking. You use them to tell yourself that something you know is wrong really isn't that bad. **Thinking errors** help you convince yourself that your abusive behavior is really OK, or that it's somebody else's fault.

Thinking errors are mental games you play with yourself. They allow you to make excuses for your behavior. **Thinking errors** allow you to put the responsibility for your behavior on to someone else.

Most people's behavior is based on feelings, not on logical decisions. If you don't take care of your angry, hurt or vulnerable feelings in a positive way, those feelings will stay inside you. You will probably end up using **thinking errors** to let you do bad things to people to try to get rid of those feelings or cover them up.

Abusing power is a **thinking error.** So is telling most of the truth, but leaving some parts out. So is blaming someone else for your actions. Making your offending behavior seem not very important is a **thinking error**, too.

Thinking errors don't just show up with offending behavior. Once you know what they are, you'll probably find you've been using **thinking errors** at school, with your parents or with your friends. You may start noticing when other people use **thinking errors**.

Regardless of where they happen, **thinking errors** are always a way to distort the truth. They are a way of not taking responsibility for your behavior.

Here are some of the **thinking errors** the kids in this book used when they were offending. Do any of them sound familiar to you? You'll find a list of **thinking errors** in the Appendix.

ADAM *"I used all of 'em – the lying, re-defining, which is changing the truth around a little bit. Making excuses for something I did. Minimizing – making the offense not as big as it was. Maximizing – making it bigger than it was. Blaming other people for what I did."*

PAUL *"My thinking errors were lack of empathy, power plays, anger, lying. Lying by omission – that's when you tell part of the truth, but you're still lying. Another one I use is procrastination. I was procrastinating by not telling the group what really happened in my offense. I use procrastination a lot, like with my chores, my homework."*

STACE *"When I molested my foster brother I told myself I was only doing what my mom taught me. (That thinking error is justification.) And she did teach me to use sex for everything, but it still didn't make it right to do what I did. He didn't want it, and I forced it on him."*

ELI *"Mostly lack of empathy. I never gave a thought how anybody else might feel. I was just worried about myself."*

BEN *"Minmizing my actions. I justified what I did by saying 'she was flirting with me.' 'She wanted me to.' I made it sound like my raping her was her fault.*

I've learned that thinking errors are the things that give me the OK to offend. If I can rationalize why I need to offend, then I'll offend."

DEL *"When I was offending, it was mainly assuming that my victims would like whatever I did to them. Thinking errors reinforce your sex offender behavior. I thought they would make me look good, but really they made me look bad."*

ALEXIS *"The thinking error I used was lying. Then I told lies to cover up those lies. And I lied to myself, telling myself I wasn't going to get caught."*

KYLE *"Playing the victim. My mom was – still is – a practicing alcoholic. When I was living with her she was out at the bar every night. I felt, 'She doesn't care about me, so let's do something so she'll notice me.' I tried it. I got away with it, so I just kept on going until it built up, 'til I had 7 victims."*

BARRY *"The main one was super-*

optimism, 'I'll never be caught.' Also, I used justification: 'Well, I was offended, so that gives me the right to go out and offend, to get my power back.'

And, I don't know what it would be called, but I covered up. I used to watch 911 with my mom. Every time there would be a sex offender on I would always say, 'How disgusting. How can somebody do that? Those people should be shot and killed.' When, in fact, I was offending then, myself."

ERIC *"You name it. I did a lot of shifting of focus, blaming the victim. 'Oh, look at the way she's dressed. She wants it.' Excuse-making: 'If she don't want me to, she'll tell me no,' even though I knew she was already saying no by her body language and actions. If she didn't actually say no, I would tell myself that gave me permission to go ahead."*

You can see that there are a lot of different kinds of thinking errors. Maybe you've used some of them for years. Maybe this is the first you've heard that this kind of thinking is what makes it possible for you to hurt other people.

You will be spending a lot of time learning about your thinking errors in treatment. You may even get tired of hearing about them. But learning about thinking errors is very important. Thinking errors are the mental tools that allow you to offend. Learning to identify and change your thinking errors – and the feelings that led to them – is a way of getting rid of those tools. It will also help reduce your desire to offend and help you get your life on track.

??? ▶

Questions:

Explain in your own words what thinking errors are.

Why do you need to learn about thinking errors in your treatment program?

What thinking errors did you use the most that allowed you to hurt your victims?

What thinking errors do you use in your day-to-day life?

What thinking errors do you notice other people using?

Why do you think people use thinking errors?

Why do you think Adam used maximizing (making things seem bigger then they were) as a thinking error about his offending?

Words to Remember:

There are a lot of words to remember from this section. Please turn to the Appendix to get definitions for these thinking errors:

Assuming, Blaming,

Catastrophizing, Excuse-making,

Image, Lack of empathy,

Lying, Lying by omission,

Minimizing, Maximizing,

Procrastinating, Redefining,

Shifting focus, Super optimism,

Victim-playing

Chapter 16: Changing Your Thinking Errors

"The first part of learning empathy is identifying your own feelings.

After that, you begin to think how someone else might feel if you hurt them."

When you use thinking errors for a long time, they become a habit. You use them when you don't need to. You use them to avoid accepting the consequences of your behavior. Using thinking errors twists the way you see life. You start thinking about everything as if you were a criminal.

It can take a long time to get out of the habit of using thinking errors. The first step is to figure out what thinking errors are and why they are wrong. Then you figure out which thinking errors you use the most. Next is figuring out how to change them.

Here are what some of these offenders went through in trying to learn about and change their thinking errors.

ALEXIS *"I learned that if you do tell a lie, you're going to have to keep on making lies over and over again to justify that one lie. And also, that everyone finds out about the lies."*

PAUL *"In this program, if you do something against the rules, you have to write a report listing the thinking errors you used. ... Say you hit somebody. You write down what the problem was, the thinking errors you used and the things you told yourself to support those thinking errors. That's the way I learned what my thinking errors are."*

ELI *"My biggest thinking error was not feeling **empathy** for my victims. The first part of learning **empathy** is identifying your own feelings. After that, you begin to think how someone else might feel if you hurt them. But if you're not good at feeling your own feelings, you're definitely not going to be good at knowing how someone else feels.*

For me this was a long, long process. I learned a little bit about it each week. I think I reached my height when I found out that a good friend of mine had been abused. One night I just started crying for what happened to her."

BEN *"**Empathy** for my victim was the hardest thing for me to get. After I offended my victims a few times, I didn't even think about them anymore. They just became an object. I had* *to learn to not objectify them, to start seeing them as people I was hurting.*

I was just spinning my wheels for a long time. Months. Then one night I was writing down my offenses from my victim's point of view and I just broke down and cried. It was kinda hard, but it helped me out a lot."

MONTE *"One of the biggest things that's helped me in learning victim empathy is role-playing. I've played the victim while another kid played me – the offender. I got to see how my victims probably felt. It made me feel real small."*

Empathy means understanding how someone else is feeling, as if you yourself were feeling that same way. Say you've played a lot of basketball and have won and lost a lot of games. A good friend of yours calls you up after losing a close game. You can have **empathy** for your friend because you know how he or she is feeling.

The opposite of empathy is disregarding or hurting someone else's feelings. Not having **empathy** for your victims is a thinking error because you are refusing to acknowledge that you hurt your victims.

As Eli said, a first step towards learning empathy is being able to identify the different feelings that are inside you.

Monte said that **role-playing** helped him learn empathy. **Role-playing** is like a little skit that you do in treatment. You might play the part of the victim, the offender, or even

your parents. Like Monte said, role-playing is a way to get in touch with how other people feel. It's also a way to get in touch with different feelings that are inside you.

ERIC *"My biggest excuse always was, 'I've done this with her lots of times and she never said no. Why should it be different this time? It ain't that bad. I just made her do this or do that.'*

*But when I get rid of my thinking errors I realize she has these rights, these **limits** and **boundaries**, and I have to respect them. And that I have no excuse for not respecting them."*

The idea of **boundaries** might be hard to understand at first, but look at it this way. People often use fences to mark off their yard from their neighbor's yard. In a way, the fence says, "I have a right to control everything on my side of the fence. You have a right to control everything on your side of the fence."

People don't come with fences, but they have the same kind of boundaries that need to be respected. When you touch someone without their permission, it's the same as crossing their fence. You are trespassing on that person's personal space.

You can cross someone's **boundaries** by standing too close to them, by making suggestive comments to them, or by rubbing up against sexual parts of their body when you are "just fooling around." Some people are good at telling you when you are crossing their **boundar**y. Some people are not. Sex offenders often take advantage of people who don't or can't say when their **boundaries** are being crossed.

Just because someone doesn't tell you you are crossing their **boundary** doesn't mean that everything is OK. Maybe they don't say anything because you intimidate them, or maybe they want to please you, or maybe they're too young to say what they feel in words.

Sex offenders have not learned to respect other people's **boundaries**. Maybe it is because their **boundaries** were violated when they were growing up. Maybe it's because their parents were confused about their own **boundaries**. Some sex offenders might have learned from their families that ignoring other people's **boundaries** is OK.

In treatment, you will learn to understand and respect that EVERYONE has **boundaries**, whether they say so or not, and that these **boundaries** must be respected.

Questions:

What are ways you can change the thinking errors that you use most often?

Describe what it means to have empathy for someone.

What is role-playing? If you've ever done it, what has it taught you?

What are boundaries?

Do children have boundaries? Do older people? Do babies?

What are some of your boundaries?

Why is it important to respect people's boundaries?

Have your boundaries ever been ignored? What did that feel like?

Words to Remember:

Empathy

Role-playing

Limits

Boundaries

Respect

Chapter 17:
Find the Thinking Errors

"I had thought I was sly,

that I wouldn't get caught.

Once the police got involved,

it changed my attitude,

real quick."

Here are some stories some offenders have told about how they were caught. Can you find the thinking errors in their stories? Use the list that's provided in the Appendix to help you remember all the different thinking errors. If you are in a group, you might all want to do this together. That way you can discuss which thinking errors the different offenders used.

KYLE *"My cousin was my victim. She told her mom, who is my aunt. She told my dad. He asked me if I had a problem and I told him 'no.' Then my aunt called the children's protection services number. They contacted the police, and the police came to school and arrested me.*

It was terrifying. They called me to go to the principal's office. The police were there, and told me why. They read me my rights. They walked me out to the car, searched me,

handcuffed me and took me to the detention center.

I had thought I was sly, that I wouldn't get caught. Once the police got involved, it changed my attitude, real quick."

BARRY *"One of my victims told her friend. Her friend told her mom. It all just snowballed. I denied it, but my victim kept saying it happened. Then CSD got involved.*

I was really angry. I had offended that victim lots and lots of times before and she never said anything. In my mind I had told myself she wanted it, so why is she telling now?"

DEL *"At first I told the least I could, just to get me off the hook. Being in the same office with a police officer and a counselor made me feel really insecure. It took all the power away from me that I wanted."*

BEN *"When I got interviewed, I started crying, not because of my victim, but because I didn't want to be locked up. I didn't want to be punished. I told them I offended her about 5 times, and actually I offended her a lot more than that."*

ERIC *"When my cousin told on me I wanted to kill him. I tried to con him into taking it back, and say he was lying. I didn't care what it took.*

Errata: Here are the corrected page numbers for *Tell It Like It Is*. The publisher apologizes for the error.

Contents

When I got caught again I was 17. I thought, 'Oh boy. Here we go again.' I didn't care anymore whether I got caught. I figured I'd done it so many times and they only caught me twice. Big deal."

PAUL
"My cousin told her mom. I lied at first. Her mom called the police and the county took over and prosecuted me.

I was scared. I didn't know what was going to happen. I didn't think it was that big a deal. I didn't think it was as big a crime as it is."

At least 6 or 7 thinking errors showed up in these stories. Did you spot them all?

Learning to identify and change your thinking errors is like weeding an overgrown garden. When you first start working in the garden, you can't tell the weeds from the flowers and vegetables. When you first start trying to figure out your thinking errors, you can't tell your thinking errors from your healthy thinking.

Once you know what your thinking errors are, you can start to pull them up whenever you notice them. It will take some time, but after a while you'll have less and less of them.

Like Ben said, thinking errors are what gives you the OK to sexually abuse other people. Weeding the thinking errors out of your brain is a very important step in keeping you from re-offending.

Questions:

What thinking errors showed up the most in these stories?

Why did they show up so often?

What have you learned about thinking errors that you didn't know before?

Why will fixing your thinking errors help keep you from re-offending?

Section 6.
The Abuse Cycle

Chapter 18:
What Is An Abuse Cycle?

"It's important to learn the steps in your cycle ... it's a lot easier to get out of your cycle at the beginning."

We know you didn't just wake up one day and discover you were a sex offender. Offending is the result of a long line of negative thoughts, feelings and behaviors that build up over time. These thoughts and behaviors are links in a chain that leads to your offending. Just like a bicycle chain goes around and around, your negative thoughts, feelings and behaviors form a cycle. This cycle of thoughts, feelings, beliefs and actions is called your **abuse cycle**.

Thoughts, feelings and behavior are linked together like pieces of a chain. Every action you take begins with a thought, feeling or belief. You feel hungry, you think about food, then you go find something to eat.

Your actions show the kinds of thoughts, feelings and beliefs that are in your head. When you are feeling positive about yourself, you are probably friendly, open and interested in the world. You like being with other kids your age. You feel good inside.

When you feel bad about yourself, you close off the world. You don't talk to friends. You stay in your head. You don't have fun. You may hurt yourself, or somebody else. You may destroy your belongings.

Cycles of behavior are very normal. Everyone experiences them. Some are positive. A positive cycle is when you are keeping things in focus and behaving in a way that gets your needs met without hurting anyone else.

For example, let's say you haven't been doing well on your wrestling team and the coach lets you know it. Instead of getting angry at your coach, you **take responsibility** for your poor performance. You start showing up for practice on time. You work out harder. You study other wrestlers' moves. Maybe you don't win your next match, but you've tried your best, and you feel good about that. That's a positive cycle.

Then there are negative cycles. You probably notice when someone in your family is going through a negative cycle. Inside you might think, "Oh, no. I know what happens next!"

In a negative cycle, you lose perspective. You think and act in a way that doesn't get your needs met. These are thoughts you might have in a negative cycle: "I'm always the one being blamed." "My parents don't care about me at all." "Everybody picks on me." "It's not my fault. I didn't do anything."

Because you are an offender, this kind of thinking can put you in your **abuse cycle**. That means you begin to take the mental and physical steps that end up in your sexually abusing someone.

All during your cycle you have choices. You can keep having negative thoughts and acting in negative ways. Or you can get help understanding your emotions so you can get things back in focus. Once you get things back in focus, your thinking will clear up. You might still be irritated or a little down, but you will be out of your abuse cycle.

If you stay in your negative thinking and don't deal with the real emotions within you, you will stay in your abuse cycle. The next step is using thinking errors. Thinking errors keep you in your abuse cycle. Your behaviors will

follow your thinking. You may begin to isolate. You may bully other kids.

If you don't get help, your behaviors will be harder to control. You might begin to groom a potential victim. Grooming is when you start giving someone extra attention, gifts or candy so that he or she will trust you and will be easier for you to abuse. When you are grooming someone, that means you are in high cycle. High cycle is when you are close to sexually abusing someone.

Sex offenders often deny they have a cycle. Some think it is abnormal to have a cycle. Others deny it because they don't believe they have the power to change their cycle. They want to believe their offending behavior "just happened."

In treatment, you will learn to understand your abuse cycle. You will learn to identify your warning signs – such as staying in your room a lot, or bullying your younger brother, or starting to groom someone. You will learn how to interrupt your abuse cycle so you won't offend again.

Here, Barry explains what a cycle might be like:

BARRY *"Cycles can be different for each person. There could be a step where you really have low self-worth. There could be a step where you isolate yourself, or where you go into a deviant fantasy.*

Usually I know if I'm in high cycle, but a lot of offenders don't. Grooming and fantasies are one or two of my steps before I offend. I know that when I start getting into those behaviors, I'm really high into cycle. I'm coming close to offending.

It's important to learn the steps in your cycle. That way, you can know when you are going into cycle, and learn ways to get yourself out. It's a lot easier to get out of your cycle at the beginning. When you're in high cycle it's really hard to get out."

At first, the idea of an **abuse cycle** might be hard to "get." Once you start paying attention to your behavior, you will get a clearer idea of your positive and negative cycles. From there, your group and counselor can help you understand the idea of an **abuse cycle**. The more you understand what an abuse cycle is in general, the easier it will be for you to understand and change your own abuse cycle.

Questions:

How do you feel when you are in a positive cycle?

How do you feel when you are in a negative cycle?

Do you understand what an abuse cycle is? Can you explain it in your own words?

Do you think you have an abuse cycle? Do you understand it?

Words to Remember:

Abuse cycle

Grooming

High cycle

Take responsibility

Warning signs

Chapter 19:
How Do I Know When I'm Going Into My Cycle?

"For me, my cycle starts out with a problem. If I break-up with a girlfriend, get in a fight, get fired from a job, mess up in school, get in a fight with my parents, that's the first step."

One thing that triggers a lot of offenders' cycles is when they ignore their feelings or feel that others don't respect their feelings.

The offenders in this book didn't know what an abuse cycle was when they went into treatment. Now they have all learned a lot about their cycles. Here they explain how they know when they are going into cycle. *Note:* Barry talks about having **deviant fantasies**. Deviant sexual fantasies are fantasies in which you get sexual pleasure from hurting or offending someone. We'll talk more about fantasies in Section 7.

BEN *"I can tell by ways that I act – like making fun of people, getting really angry, isolating myself."*

BARRY *"When I'm in cycle, I use grooming tactics. I spend a lot of extra time with one kid, the kid I want to offend. I give her candy or toys. Most of my victims are female. I become like a father or big brother figure toward them, so I can get their trust. Then it's easier to offend them.*

*I know I'm going into high cycle when I start talking about sexual stuff a lot. I tell sexual jokes, or fantasize about different ways to have sex. Or I start having **deviant fantasies**. I think about who I can offend, or how I can offend them."*

ELI *"I know I'm in cycle when I start pushing, shoving or punching my brother. I don't talk to anybody about my feelings. I **isolate** myself."*

YVONNE *"I know my warning signs. I don't come out of my room. I don't talk to people. I don't talk to my friends. I withdraw. I don't go to school."*

ADAM *"I'll know I'm in cycle because I get really moody. I'll be upset all the time. I stay away from everybody. I don't talk."*

DEL *"When I'm in cycle, I start spending time alone with the person I want to offend. I manipulate a lot of rules. I shut down in my group and I won't talk. I'll start acting like I'm the one getting victimized, even when I'm not."*

PAUL *"My cycle starts when I'm in a down mood. When I'm angry, upset or depressed."*

You can see that every offender has a cycle, but every offender's cycle is not the same. At one point in his cycle, Eli starts pushing his younger brother around. Yvonne will start to spend a lot of time in her room. Del **shuts down** in his group. When you **shut down** it means you stop talking and listening to what others say to you. Eli isolates himself, that is, he stops seeing friends and spends most of his time alone.

Remember, your cycle isn't just one behavior or one feeling. You cycle is made up of a string of different behaviors. It's important to figure out all the different steps in your cycle. Then you will be able to identify when you are in cycle, and learn to do things to get yourself out.

Questions:

What do you do when you feel bad about yourself? Do you isolate yourself from other people? Are you mean to younger kids? Do you drink or use drugs? Do you act like a big shot, or put on some other "image"?

What kinds of events or feelings can put you in cycle?

How do you act when you are on the path to offending someone?

What have you seen other offenders do when they go into their cycles?

Words to Remember:

Abuse cycle

Deviant fantasies

Shut down

Isolate

Chapter 20:
Drugs and Alcohol

Drugs and/or alcohol play an important part in some offenders' cycles. Drugs and alcohol cloud your judgment. They make it easier for you to use thinking errors, the mind tricks you use to make abusing and inappropriate behavior seem OK.

Some offenders abuse when they are high. Afterwards, when they've come down, they pretend their behavior never happened, or that it wasn't "that bad." They think, "Oh, I was just drunk (or high). It didn't mean anything."

Drugs and alcohol cover up your true feelings. They make you act like you are happy. Often, for a short time, they can make you feel like you are "somebody." But underneath, your real feelings may be anger, sadness, fear, disappointment, hurt or even self-hate.

It's important to stay away from drugs and alcohol during treatment. Your group or your counselor may have a rule about that, or it might be part of your probation. It's a good idea to stay away from drugs and alcohol after treatment, too. Sex offenders already have a problem with unclear thinking. Drugs and alcohol just make that problem worse.

JAY *"Drugs and alcohol covered up a lot of feelings for me. They made everything seem fine. When I offended, I drank. It made it seem like I wasn't doing anything wrong. Drugs and alcohol were a big part of my cycle."*

PAUL *"When I was offending I was drinking, doing all different types of drugs. I did drugs on the weekends and when I babysat.*

I think the drugs and alcohol had a lot to do with my not having a clear mind. I wasn't really paying attention to what was going on. I didn't care what anyone thought. I just went, 'This is what I'm going to do, and I don't care what anyone thinks.' Then I did it.

When offenders use drugs and/or alcohol, their brain isn't working straight. They give up control over what they do. You're more straight-minded when you're clean and sober. You have a lot better judgment."

Questions:

Have you ever watched someone who was high when you weren't? What was their thinking like?

Do you think sex offenders should stay away from drugs and alcohol during treatment? Why?

Are drugs and alcohol part of your abuse cycle? If so, in what way do they affect your behavior?

If you got addicted to a drug or alcohol, how long would that addiction satisfy you? When you stopped getting pleasure from the drug or alcohol, what would you turn to?

Note: If drugs and alcohol are a problem for you, read Miguel's story. It's in Chapter 45.

Chapter 21: Using Deterrents

"When I first got here, I didn't use deterrents. I didn't care if I got out of my cycle or not. But now I do care. I've hurt too many people. I don't want to re-offend. That's why I use these deterrents."

Once you figure out the different parts of your abuse cycle, you can create **deterrents** for yourself. **Deterrents** are things you do to get yourself out of cycle. **Deterrents** can be things like talking to someone else, putting pictures in your head, or even playing basketball.

When you use **deterrents**, you are taking control of yourself. You are not letting your feelings or your past or bad habits control you.

Deterrents work. When you use them, you feel good about yourself. You feel that you are in control, instead of being controlled by circumstances, other people or your feelings.

Here are some deterrents that have worked for these offenders.

BEN *"Leaving the situation is a really good thing to do if you're at the beginning of your cycle. If you're getting angry, you can walk away from the person who's making you angry. You can go talk to someone else.*

I also say things to myself like, 'If you re-offend, you can go to prison. Then you could be offended.'

Deterrents have to be real. They have to be something you're really afraid of. I'm afraid of going to prison, so saying that works for me."

BARRY *"Deterrents are different for each person. For me, I picture a little 8 X 8 jail cell. I imagine myself being in that cell. I don't want to be there, because I really don't like jail.*

There was a kid who went through this program successfully. After he got out, one of his victim's relatives killed him. That's always in my mind. That's another deterrent."

Actually, fear of being caught or of being hurt by a family member of your victim isn't by itself a very strong deterrent. You were probably afraid of being caught at some point in your cycle, but other feelings and thinking errors allowed you to abuse anyway.

Negative deterrents must be used with powerful, positive deterrents. That way you not only know what to avoid, but you also have a strong picture of the kind of life you want to have for yourself. Here are some examples of some positive deterrents.

MONTE *"Let's say I get grounded. I may be so angry that I start going into cycle. I try to calm down and look at all sides. I say to myself, 'OK, you messed up. That's why you're grounded. You need to accept it. You need to take responsibility for your actions.' Other times I may go and talk to somebody. That helps too."*

JAY *"I use positive self-talk to get me out of my cycle. I used a lot of negative self-talk when I offended. So I try and do the opposite.*

If I'm isolating myself, I tell myself to go be with people. You can still be alone in a crowd, but for me it helps. I talk to my parole officer, or a support person."

Do you know what **self-talk** is? **Self-talk** is conversation you have inside your head. Self-talk can be positive or negative. Jay used negative self-talk when he offended to make his behavior seem OK. Now he uses positive self-talk to lift himself up when he gets down.

ADAM *"When I'm having a problem, a fight or something, I try and find someone to talk to about how I feel. I go do something I'm good at, like sports, until I feel better about myself. Then I go back and talk to someone about what happened.*

YVONNE *"I know my warning signs. I don't come out of my room. I don't talk to people. I don't talk to my friends. I withdraw. I don't go to school.*

But I don't go into cycle as much now. I don't have time to dwell on things, to muster the energy to offend. I have too much studying to do."

DEL *"If I'm going into cycle, I go talk to someone, to staff or a peer. I look into the future, and think what will happen to me if I stay in cycle. I think about positive ideas."*

PAUL *"If I think I'm in my cycle, I'll try and do something constructive. I'll stay in my room, listen to the radio, try and cool down. I call my grandma every week, that helps. She helps me with things I can do to get out of a bad mood. Having plans, doing stuff with my friends. That helps too."*

Deterrents work for you, not against you. Using deterrents helps you feel more in control of your behavior and your life. Other people can give you ideas for deterrents, but *nobody* can make you use them, except you. Each time you use a deterrent and it works, feel proud of yourself. You are a step closer to taking control of your life and outgrowing sexual offending.

Questions:

Do you understand what a *deterrent* is?

Have you ever tried to get out of your cycle?

What deterrents worked for you? Which ones didn't?

Are there times when you just want to stay in cycle? What keeps you there? Is there someone you can go to when that happens?

Words to Remember:

Deterrents

Negative self-talk

Positive self-talk

Chapter 22:
Staying Out of Cycle

"I think a lot of times now I don't get into my cycle as much, because I let people know how I feel now. I didn't do that before."

Your abuse cycle has probably become a habit. Habits aren't easy to break. Like other habits, before you can break it, you first need to recognize it. Once you know what your cycle is, you may have to use a deterrent a lot of times before it really works. You may work hard to get yourself out of cycle, then slide right back in.

Here, some offenders talk about the hard parts of getting out – and staying out – of their abuse cycle.

BEN *"Anger's a big part of my cycle. It's one of my hardest things, because it's so hard to get out of. When I'm really angry, I just want to hurt somebody. I could start punching on someone, and not want to stop.*

The thing that pushes me to the next step in my cycle is usually anger. I try to get out of my cycle, and anger just keeps yanking me right back in."

YVONNE *"I don't take so much from my mom anymore, and believe it or not that helps me stay out of my cycle. I tell her 'No.' I don't sit there and take her yelling at me anymore.*

The way I used to be was like a little mouse with a shy little voice. Now, I'm like, 'I've got a voice, and you're going to hear it. You're going to know my opinions, my viewpoint.' That makes me feel a whole lot stronger, like I have some power. It keeps me out of cycle."

MONTE *"There are times when I know I'm in cycle. I keep on saying to myself, 'I can get out of this without help,' so I don't go talk to anybody. Or I don't get concerned about it, because I'm worried about other things in my life. It's not good when I don't pay attention to my cycle."*

ELI *"While I was in group, I let myself go completely through my cycle. I almost re-offended. I was at a party where there was other, younger kids. There were a couple chances, but the kids went away. I think I just got lucky.*

After that, I got smart. I told my probation officer, then I told group. That helped a lot. I haven't gone that far into cycle since."

JAY *"Figuring out my cycle is confusing. I know some of my behaviors, but some of them I don't see. I don't know which step goes where. When I think about the past, it seems I was pretty much in cycle every day."*

DEL *"When I'm really in my cycle, there's nothing I can do to get myself out. When I want to be in cycle, I can't get me out. Someone else has to sit down and talk to me."*

Once you become good at recognizing the danger signs that let you know you are in your cycle, it will be easier to get out of your cycle.

But just because you got yourself out of your cycle once or twice doesn't mean you're home free. Staying out of cycle will take effort, time and lots of tries. Sometimes what you try will work, and sometimes it won't, at least not the first time.

It will help a lot if you develop high expectations for keeping yourself out of cycle. This is more than "wishful thinking." It happens after you have found yourself in cycle and have been able to get yourself out. By doing this you will build up your confidence and self-respect.

Expressing your true feelings, recognizing your danger signs, using deterrents and having high expectations will help you stay out of cycle. It will help a lot if you have someone you can talk to when you feel like you may be going into cycle.

Questions:

Have you tried to stay out of cycle? Was it easy or difficult?

What pulls you back into your cycle?

How do you fight it when something pulls you into your cycle?

Chapter 23: Getting Help

"A lot of learning about my cycle is from living at the group home. They know a lot of the warning signs about going into cycle. They'll let me know if I'm in cycle. They'll talk to me, help me out."

Other people can be a big help in keeping you out of your cycle. Other kids in your group might know when you're in cycle, even if you don't. People in your group home might know. Or your counselor. Parents can also learn to recognize the signs. Talk to them. They can help you become aware of when you're in cycle. They can help you get out.

Remember: Everybody in the group has an abuse cycle, not just you!

BARRY *"When some people first get here, they don't know when they're in cycle. But after you've been here a while, you can tell. You can talk to them, show them what they're doing."*

MONTE *"A lot of learning about my cycle is from living at the group home. They deal with a lot of sex offenders. They know a lot of the warning signs about going into cycle. They'll let me know if I'm in cycle."*

ADAM *"In group, we talk about cycles. Then we talk about how we've acted. The leaders tell us, 'This has to change, or you'll re-offend.'*

We talk about ways to change our behaviors, because just looking at them won't change them. You gotta do something real, like use deterrents. I go through my deterrents every day. I sit down, talk to somebody. I say, 'This is the person I want to be. How do I get there?'"

When you interrupt your cycle you are changing your offending habits. It's a good and powerful feeling. It shows that you can be in charge of yourself, that you can act differently than you did in the past. It tells you that you can make good decisions for yourself. It says you are becoming someone who chooses not to abuse.

Here's what one young offender says about how using deterrents makes him feel:

ADAM *"Using deterrents makes me feel good. I know if I can keep it up, I won't reoffend again. I don't know for a fact that I will or not re-offend. I'm hoping that I don't."*

I keep telling myself everyday that I'm going to succeed, that I'm not going to re-offend. Knowing that my deterrents work makes me feel good because I can do something else besides sports and feel good about it."

It might be hard at first to go to someone for help when you feel like you are going into your cycle. But think about it this way: When you start to feel like you're getting pneumonia, don't you go get some medicine for it, or go to the doctor? Instead of the pneumonia, your problem is being a sex offender. It only makes sense to go get help when you feel symptoms coming on. That's called taking responsibility for yourself.

Questions:

Have you ever tried talking to someone when you thought you were going into cycle? Did it help you out?

Who are good people for you to talk to when you are having trouble staying out of cycle?

How has it felt when you have gotten yourself out of cycle?

Words to Remember:

Re-offend

Taking responsibility

Warning signs

Section 7. Fantasies

Chapter 24: Appropriate, Inappropriate or Deviant fantasies

"At first I thought that we – sex offenders – must have the worst sexual fantasies of anybody around. And we do. But I also found out that sexual fantasies are part of most people's lives, and that healthy fantasies are OK."

You may already know what a fantasy is. A **fantasy** is a story or scene you make up in your mind. It's thinking about and picturing something happening. Sometimes people are not even aware that they might be fantasizing in the "back of their minds." It doesn't always take a lot of attention or concentration. You can have different kinds of fantasies. You may fantasize about good things you'd like to have happen to you. You may fantasize about bad things you are afraid might happen to you.

A **sexual fantasy** is when sex is a part – or all – of the story you make up. Sexual fantasies can be healthy or unhealthy.

Here's the difference. In healthy fantasies, the people in the story:

- Have a relationship that includes more than just sex.

- Are of equal or appropriate age and maturity.

- Have equal power.

- Freely consent to the sexual activity. (Another way to say that is that the activity was **consensual**. **Consensual** means both people have free will and agree to the activity. Both people understand what being sexually active means and how it will affect them. **Consensual** means both parties have equal power to say "No.")

- In no way hurt anyone or force someone to do something against their will.

The most healthy sexual fantasies have all these parts. They are also called **appropriate**

sexual fantasies. Almost everyone has them, and they're part of a normal, healthy sexual life.

Inappropriate sexual fantasies are fantasies where one or more of those parts we just listed is missing. For example, maybe the person in your fantasy is your girlfriend, but you pressure her into doing something sexual that you know she doesn't want to do. That's an **inappropriate sexual fantasy**.

Another example of an **inappropriate fantasy** is where the person in your fantasy is age-appropriate and agrees to the sexual activity, but you use her or him as a **sexual object**. That means you have no relationship with him or her, that you are using the person just for sex and don't care about the real person inside.

Lots of people have inappropriate fantasies, not just sex offenders. But unhealthy, inappropriate fantasies are a special problem for sex offenders because many sex offenders act out their fantasies in real life in ways that hurt other people. When they don't act out one particular fantasy, they get used to imagining people as objects, without feelings of their own, things they can use for sex. Then they are ready to abuse whoever happens to be available, even when they don't match a particular fantasy.

Inappropriate sexual fantasies train your brain and body to respond to inappropriate sexual situations. They are one link in a chain of thoughts and behaviors that make up your abuse cycle. Making your sexual fantasies appropriate is one step in breaking your offending cycle.

A more serious level of inappropriate fantasies are **deviant fantasies**. **Deviant fantasies** are fantasies where you get sexual pleasure from hurting the other person in your fantasy, or from violating his or her will. All fantasies about sexual abuse are deviant. Fantasies about having sex with children, or peers who are drunk or drugged, or anyone who is mentally disabled are deviant.

Almost everyone at some point has an unhealthy or deviant sexual thought. The important thing is what you do with that thought. Do you take the thought in an unhealthy direction, or do you change it or stop it?

Having deviant fantasies is a link in many offenders' cycles. If you are having deviant fantasies, and especially if you are enjoying them, you are probably in your abuse cycle. You may be in high cycle. High cycle is where you start taking the steps to sexually assault someone.

Here Ben, Eli, Jay and Kyle help explain the difference between healthy and appropriate fantasies and inappropriate and deviant fantasies.

BEN *"Healthy fantasies are age-appropriate. That means the people in the fantasy aren't a lot younger or older than you are. In a healthy fantasy, you can't manipulate the person. You have to have a relationship, not just be out to use her for one thing. You can't have a forceful rape."*

ELI *"Deviant fantasies are having a fantasy where you're hurting somebody, or having sex with your sister or your mother. In appropriate fantasies, you have to get to know the person first, then go into the sexual part."*

JAY *"It's real important to know the difference between appropriate and inappropriate fantasies. Because if you don't know, you're going to offend again. You gotta see both sides of a person—the physical and the emotional. If you just see a person as an object, to you all they're there for is sex."*

KYLE *"An inappropriate fantasy is when you don't have consent. Or the person in your fantasy doesn't have a name. A deviant fantasy is when the person is only a torso. In a proper fantasy, there's consent. The person has a face, a name, and all the body parts are there."*

Having inappropriate fantasies is a beginning step on the way to offending. Having deviant fantasies brings you even closer to assaulting someone. If you have these kinds of fantasies, it is very important to deal with them in your treatment.

Here offenders talk about how inappropriate or deviant fantasies played a role in their abuse cycles.

BEN *"When you masturbate to deviant fantasies, it backs 'em up. It's like physical contact. You replay that fantasy time after time after time. It's*

like rehearsing before you offend. Your offense don't have to be related to the fantasy, the fantasy still backs it up."

JAY *"My fantasies were deviant, raping my victims, stuff like that. I thought about my fantasies a lot. I looked at girls as objects.*

ELI *"I would have a lot of fantasies with my victims in 'em. With masturbation, they played a big part in my offending. My mind basically said, 'it's OK to offend.'"*

BARRY *"I fantasized about actually doing the things I did in my fantasies. One of my fantasies was of fondling young children, because they didn't have any pubic hair. I picked victims that would fit into my fantasies. Most of my victims were real young."*

ALEXIS *"Before I molested I would watch pornography. Then I would think of a guy that I liked, and would imagine us having sex. It would make me want to do it with someone. Eventually I'd go offend one of my victims."*

BEN *"The way fantasies go is, first you have some that are consensual. Then, for offenders anyway, they become deviant. They go into a rape, or to children.*

If you are an offender, your fantasies just keep getting more deviant. Unless you do treatment, you can't change your fantasies at all. I know if I was not doing treatment, I would still be having deviant fantasies."

BARRY *"One of my fantasies was putting the face of a 9 or 10-year-old on the body of a 17-year-old. I told myself that was OK, because in the fantasy it was an older, adult female body, and we had consensual sexual contact.*

In fact, that was a deviant fantasy, because I was taking a part of a young child and putting it on parts of an older woman."

Remember how we talked about the link between your feelings, thoughts and behaviors? Fantasies are a good example of those links, how your mind creates scenes (or thoughts) that you later end up acting out. Learning the difference between healthy and unhealthy fantasies is a step toward controlling your sexual fantasies. Learning to control your fantasies will give you more power over your behavior.

Questions:

What is a sexual fantasy?

What makes a fantasy healthy or appropriate?

What is the difference between appropriate and inappropriate fantasies?

What is the difference between inappropriate and deviant fantasies?

Looking at the statements about inappropriate and deviant fantasies by these young offenders, do you notice any thinking errors?

How are inappropriate and deviant fantasies part of an offender's cycle?

What can happen if you don't learn to interrupt appropriate or deviant fantasies?

Can a person become addicted to fantasies? What should they do if they are?

Words to Remember:

Appropriate fantasies

Inappropriate fantasies

Consensual

Deviant fantasies

Sex object

Chapter 25:
Not Easy to Talk About, Are They?

"It's always scary [to talk about your fantasies in group]. Because you're afraid that people in group will think of you as really low."

One of the first steps to learning how to change your fantasies is to learn about how they are right now. In some treatment programs, offenders have to keep a record of their sexual fantasies. They write down all the sexual fantasies they had in a period of time. That way they learn if they have inappropriate or deviant fantasies, and what **triggers** them., or sets them off.

If you are in one-on-one counseling, your counselor will probably ask you to talk about your fantasies. If you are in group treatment, you may be asked to talk about your fantasies in group.

Talking about fantasies isn't easy. Fantasies are very private, and it's hard to show private parts of yourself to others. If you struggle with inappropriate or deviant fantasies, it may be hard to share this with the group.

But talking about your fantasies is important. It brings them out into the open. It lets you see if they are truly inappropriate or deviant. It lets you see how they are part of your cycle. It helps you learn how to change them.

As Barry says, "You need to talk about your fantasies so you understand which ones are OK and which ones aren't."

This is how these offenders feel when they have to talk about their fantasies.

BEN *"I don't really have a problem with it. Some I didn't want to talk about, but I did. Other kids do not want to talk about their fantasies at all."*

ELI *"It's hard, but it helps to talk about your fantasies. In your head you may know that a fantasy was wrong. But when you express it verbally, your mind really gets it.*

A while back, I had a deviant fantasy. When I had to talk about that, it was real tough. I told my parole officer, then my counselor, then I told the group. I don't think I've had one since."

BARRY *"It's always scary. Because you're afraid that people in group will think of you as really low. As it is, we're about the lowest people in the state, anyway.*

Some people in the group get aroused when

you talk about your fantasies. That's scary too, because in a way that's re-victimizing your victim. It's scary to think, if I read this fantasy, are people going to get aroused?"

Talking about inappropriate or deviant fantasies in front of others can bring up a lot of feelings – fear, shame, confusion, guilt. You may experience arousal, or be afraid that others will respond that way.

If you are feeling afraid, you might want to ignore or skip over your unhealthy fantasies, and just talk about the healthy ones. This will backfire, because you will still be holding on to the deviant fantasy. Your shame will still be controlling you.

Even though it's difficult, it's important to talk about fantasies in your treatment. It's also important to talk about the feelings you have when you talk about your fantasies. If you don't talk about your fantasies, they can get stronger and stronger. This will push you toward re-offending.

Questions:

Have you talked about your inappropriate fantasies in group or to your counselor? If so, how did that make you feel?

Does it help you to talk about your fantasies? Why?

How does it make you feel when other kids talk about their deviant fantasies?

When you get aroused listening to other kids' fantasies, how do you handle it?

Word to Remember:

Trigger

Chapter 26: Interrupting Deviant Fantasies

"I've learned to block them out, to put something else in my head, like another thought. Not a girl, but sports or a good memory."

Learning to **interrupt** your inappropriate and deviant fantasies is important. It will teach you that you can have power over your thoughts and your behavior. **Interrupting** your fantasies also can help interrupt your abuse cycle.

You will need "tools" to learn how to interrupt or change your inappropriate or deviant fantasies. The tools may include things like putting a parent or a police officer in your fantasy, or learning to do something active to stop the fantasy, like going out for a walk. Another tool is learning how to switch your mind to another channel.

Your group and your counselor can give you more ideas on tools you can use to change inappropriate fantasies or interrupt deviant fantasies.

Different tools work for different people. You may have to try several different tools to find what works for you. Once you learn to interrupt your fantasies, you will feel more in control of yourself.

Here are tools these offenders use to interrupt or change their deviant fantasies.

KYLE *"If I start having a deviant fantasy, I make it appropriate. If it's a younger victim, I make 'em older. I make 'em have all their body parts, a face, a name and consent."*

BEN *"Sometimes they have you put a rubber band around your wrist. When you start to have a fantasy, you snap it. The little pain blocks your mind. But I don't do that."*

JAY *"My brain isn't strong enough to change by itself. If I have a negative picture in there, I have to slide it out. Then I put in something else. I put in sports, or remember something good that happened. Then I look at those pictures. Sometimes that works. Sometimes it's hard, because I want to keep on with the fantasy."*

KYLE *"The only time I have fantasies is when I'm sitting down and relaxing. Or when I'm working on an assignment for group, like when you write down the details of all your offenses. I'll be thinking about what I did to my victims and I'll start having fantasies. I told group about that. They told me to put things I don't like in my fantasies, like a police officer, or my dad.*

I tried putting the police officer in my fantasy. It scared the living daylights out of me. And, well, I haven't had fantasies for quite a while now."

BEN *"I've been struggling with deviant fantasies since my last treatment. I'm starting to deal with them, but every now and then I slip back. But I know how to stop myself, how to make the fantasy appropriate."*

Once you learn what tools work for you, you can have control over your fantasies. Having control over your fantasies will give you more control over your sexually abusive behavior. When you realize that you can interrupt your inappropriate or deviant fantasies, it will give you a feeling of positive power.

Questions:

Have you tried to interrupt or change your inappropriate or deviant fantasies?

What tools work for you in interrupting your fantasies? What doesn't work?

Do you understand why some offenders have to keep a record of their sexual fantasies?

Words to Remember:

Interrupt

Tools

Section 8. Family Matters

Chapter 27: Telling Your Parents

"My mom never wanted to talk about anything. When she found out, she said, 'Oh no, not Eric.' "

It was tough to tell your parents and your family you had committed sex offenses, wasn't it. In fact, it was probably one of the hardest things you've ever had to do. Or maybe you haven't yet found the courage to tell them much of anything.

No matter how difficult our relationship with our parents is, they are very important to us. We may be angry at them, rebel against them or think they are stupid. But we still care what they think of us.

At first, most offenders don't want to tell their parents or families the truth about their offending behavior. They are afraid their parents won't love them anymore. They don't want their family to think they are bad. They don't want their parents to punish them. Many offenders remain in denial about their offending behavior because of these fears.

How did your parents or your family members react when they found out about your offenses? Were they shocked? Angry? Disappointed?

Parents don't all react the same way. Some will deny that you are an offender. They'll say things like, 'Oh, what he did wasn't that bad.' Or, 'Kids do that all the time. He was just experimenting.' Some parents will blame your victims.

Other parents can't believe it at first, but after a while they do. Some parents believe it right away. They might be shocked, angry or very sad. They may even **disown** you, want nothing to do with you for awhile.

No matter how they react at first, most parents want their child to get treatment so that this never happens again. They may offer emotional support after they get over the first shock.

This is what happened when these offenders told their parents and their families what they had done.

ERIC *"Both my parents were really hurt, really sad. They mistrusted me, were disgusted with me. All my life, my stepdad had been telling me, 'If you have a problem, come talk to me.' But I was afraid to talk to him. He had a pretty bad temper.*

My mom holds her feelings in. She never wanted to talk about anything. When she found out, she went in denial. She still is. She thinks what I did wasn't that bad. But she's slowly learning that it was."

BEN *My dad just said, 'Oh God.' That was all. He used to let me get away with anything. I figured I could get away with this, too. If the cops hadn't found out, I probably would have.*

At first my dad believed me when I minimized what I had done. He kept cussin' out the case-workers behind their backs. I said my sister wanted it, and my family believed me. They started saying she was a real slut. They thought that even after the cops told 'em the truth about what I did.

Now my dad tells me to hang in there, keep up with my treatment. But back then, he wasn't supportive at all."

DEL *"When I came into the courtroom, my mom started*

crying. She didn't want me to get locked up. She didn't know I would be getting treatment.

*I was afraid she'd **disown** me. I still am. She doesn't know my sister was one of my victims. I'm going to tell her the next time she comes.*

I'm afraid of how she'll react. I know she'll get mad or disappointed or something, which is totally OK. But if she does disown me, it's not going to hold me back from treatment. I'm prepared. I've talked to the staff, they've given me a lot of support."

JAY *"When my sister told my mom, my mom called the police. She didn't talk to me. Later I told her half the story, to get her on my side. For a while, she believed me.*

When I finally told her the truth, she didn't believe me. I told her that I had been lying. Finally she believed my sister, who was saying the same thing I was.

I didn't really worry about her rejecting me. I thought I was already rejected, because she was never around, anyway."

PAUL *"My dad's reaction was, 'All right, I'll do any-thing I can to help you.' My mom didn't want to have anything to do with me. She made me go live with my dad. It felt like she disowned me. Her attitude was, 'You messed up. You go live with your dad and take care of it.'*

My dad accepted it. He helps me with the stuff in group. He's real supportive."

YVONNE *"When my*

family found out, all hell broke loose. Everything got torn up. Nobody would talk to each other. Nobody wanted talk to me. My mom didn't want to deal with it. I didn't want to deal with it. Everybody looked at me like I was a dirty person.

I was the baby of the family. I was considered an angel, because I never did no wrong in the eyes of my father. After it came out, I was afraid that everybody in the family was going to hate me for what I did."

ADAM *"My mom was shocked, at first. She*

knew I was having a rough time, but she didn't know I was offending. She didn't realize I was hurting her kids, or people she knew.

At first I told her I didn't do anything. But then I got arrested and sent here. I wrote her and told her that I was guilty. I explained a lot of things. She came up here with my grandparents and we had a good talk."

ELI *"When my parents first found out, they didn't believe it at all.*

Then they were really upset, angry. My father was really confused. He was in a state of shock for about a week. They didn't throw me out of the family, but I couldn't live at their house anymore.

My family was really good at confronting it directly. That was a lot of help for me, too. If

*they would have tried to **minimize** what I had done, I would have done that, too."*

MONTE *"My mother wasn't*

***devastated**, but highly disappointed. She was an alcoholic, so she understood that my offending was a sickness. She knew I would work on it. She knew there was hope for me."*

BARRY *"At first I denied*

everything. My parents said, 'Oh, Barry couldn't have done that.' I was a good kid, never got in trouble.

I was afraid my dad would reject me once he knew the truth. Instead my parents said, 'OK, you come out with it, we're behind you, let's get you some treatment.'

But after I kept failing polygraphs, my dad got mad. He called me everything in the book. He couldn't figure out why I couldn't be truthful. After I failed the 6th one, my mother just broke down and cried.

After I passed my polygraph, my parents glowed like lightbulbs, because I had finally told the truth, all of it."

Just as it's hard – but important – for you to face the truth about yourself, it's hard and important for your parents to face the truth about you. Knowing that you are a sex offender probably makes your parents feel overwhelmed. They probably don't know what to do to help you change your behavior. They may feel that they have failed in raising you. They may feel helpless or think that your offending is their fault.

You aren't responsible for taking care of your parents' feelings, but you do need to respect those feelings. You may want to talk with your counselor or group about how your parents' feelings affect you. It will also help to talk to them about these feelings.

Questions:

How did you feel when you told your parents and your family about your offending? Were you scared, upset, ashamed, embarrassed, defiant?

Did you tell them the whole truth right off? If you didn't, why didn't you?

What were you most afraid to tell them? Why?

How did your parents react?

How did other people in your family react?

Did your parents or anyone in your family try to deny or minimize what you had done? Did you let them?

Words to Remember:

Disown

Emotional support

Devastated

Minimize

Polygraph

Chapter 28:
Mom, Dad and You

"My dad and I have gotten closer. Sometimes I still act like a kid, but everybody does, even my dad. But we understand where each of us is at."

Do you get along with your parents? Do you get mad at them a lot? Do they get angry at you, too?

Doing your program can change your relationship with your parents. Of course, you can't just show up for treatment. You have to participate. You have to want to change your behavior. You have to want to learn how. And you have to try.

If you "do" your treatment, you will learn to take more responsibility for your feelings and your behavior. You will stop blaming other people for your problems. You will learn to express how you feel in direct, healthy ways. You will start changing your thinking errors.

All of this means your behavior will start to change for the better. Your parents will probably notice. They will begin to rebuild trust in you. Your relationship will start to get better.

Remember that parents are just people. Many have their own problems – with drugs, alcohol, with their self-esteem or in saying what they feel. Some parents may go to a counselor for help. Some may not.

If your parents have serious problems, they may not notice when your behavior changes, even if it's for the better. They may not support what you are learning in your treatment. If you think this might happen with you, talk with your group or counselor. They can give you the support you need.

Here these young offenders explain how being in treatment changed – or didn't change – their relationship with their parents.

PAUL *"Since I've been in treatment, things with my dad have gotten better. I put forth more of an effort. Before, I was always trying to get back to my mom's. Now I'm trying to make the best of it here."*

DEL *"My relationship with my mom hasn't gotten better. It hasn't gotten worse, either. She didn't know I was rapin'. I held it in so good she didn't know. I still can't talk to her about being a sex offender. Before all this I couldn't talk to her, and I still can't. Still, she's proud of me 'cause I'm doing well in treatment and I finished school."*

ALEXIS *"Now when I get angry, I*

don't slam things, or scream at the top of my lungs. It's helped listening to how other kids handle their problems. My mom's noticed that I'm different. Whenever I'm with her, I'm a lot happier. I think my grandparents have noticed, too. We get along a lot better."

ADAM *"I think there's been some good come out of all this. My family is really dysfunctional. There's 9 people. Before, we were all against each other. This has brought us all closer together.*

My grandparents, my mom, are all supportive. My mom writes all the time. I write back. I tell her what's going on, how I'm feeling."

ELI *"I think my relationship with my parents has gotten better. I've learned to express my feelings, and there's more understanding betweeen us. After they found out about my offending, I lost their trust. But I think little by little I'm gaining it back."*

MONTE *"At first, I wasn't really participating in treatment and my mom got mad. She finally said, 'You're not helping yourself. Until you get yourself together, I'm not going to have any more contact with you.'*

That shook me up. I started getting my act together. Now we understand each other a whole lot better. We talk a lot more, we have serious discussions."

KYLE *"My dad and I have gotten closer. Both of us being in AA has been helpful, because when I drank, I did it to be with him. We don't try to be buddies like before. I sit down and talk to him like he's my father. Living with him helps too."*

YVONNE *"My family never really recovered. We can't even get together for a holiday. My one sister, she's a downright bitch. I won't talk to her no more. Things are better with my mom, though."*

Treatment won't make the problems between you and your parents disappear. But if you use the skills you learn in your treatment, your relationship with your parents will improve. You will be able to communicate what you are thinking and feeling more clearly. You will learn to take care of your feelings and respect the feelings of others. You will feel better about yourself, and act that way, too.

Questions:

How has your behavior changed since you've been in treatment?

Have your parents noticed?

Have you noticed any changes in your parents?

If your behavior has changed, has it affected your relationship with your parents? With other family members? How?

Chapter 29:
Looking at the Past

"When I was a kid, I had no power or control. All I had was rejection – being abused, thrown around by the hair on my head, getting my nose broken."

Because you don't just wake up one day and discover that you're a sex offender, we know the roots of your offending behavior are in your past. They go back to when you were little. They can begin in experiences and feelings you had when you were 3, or 6, or 8 years old.

This means that your behavior is **learned**. It also means that you can learn new ways to deal with feelings and get your needs met. In treatment you can see how to "un-learn" some negative behaviors that you learned when you were young and didn't have many choices. This time you can choose to learn more positive behaviors.

The problems you grew up with helped shape your behavior. But reasons and history aren't excuses. You can't blame your offending on a mother who was an alcoholic, or a step-father who abused you. You can't blame your offending on being poor or on your low self-esteem. Because other kids grow up with the same problems and don't sexually offend, we know that your offending was your choice. You are responsible for that behavior.

Looking at your past can help you understand why you made the choice to offend. Your past is a map of your life. It shows how you got to be where you are today.

The past can show you why you started shutting off your feelings. Or why you started feeling bad about yourself. Or when you learned that offending was "just the way people did things."

The offenders in this book all spent a lot of time exploring their past. They thought about what was going on in their lives when they first started offending. They remembered what was happening in their family, and how they felt about themselves back then.

Does any of what they say sound familiar to you?

BEN *"My parents got divorced when I was in the 6th grade. I felt helpless about that. I was getting Ds and Fs in school. That was about the time I started offending my sister. But earlier, at age 8, I was rubbing up and down her with my clothes on. That's an offense, too."*

DEL *"When I was a kid, I had no power or control. I had all rejection, being abused, thrown around by* *the hair on my head, getting my nose broken. I even saw my step-dad beat my mom with broomsticks.*

I was offended when I was 12. I started to rape that same year. I was holding all my anger at that abuse inside me. When you feel so rejected and powerless, and you are a sex offender, the only thing to do to get the power and control back is to rape."

ADAM
"I've been abused in every way possible since I was 2. I've been hit by my dad, my brothers and sisters, my mom, my grandparents. I was sexually offended twice, the first time by my father.

I was always getting into fights. I had a bad stuttering problem. I had to have tubes put in my ears, had to wear glasses. I was in special ed classes, because I had learning problems. People made fun of me because I was tall, because of all the problems I had. I felt really stupid."

MONTE
"I started abusing when I was 9. I would look at my father's pornography. My step-father was physically abusive to me. I felt really small and I had low self-esteem. When I felt really low, I would get to this certain point and I would offend. That was my way to gain back some power."

ALEXIS
"My step-dad came to live with us when I was seven. Before that it was just my mom and I, and I was used to

getting all the attention. Then my mom had my two step-brothers. My step-dad started doing drugs and he would beat on my mom. She and I fought a lot. They'd want me to babysit my brothers all the time. I was pretty angry about that, and never getting any attention from my mom."

BARRY
"The main thing, when I started offending, was rejection. By my friends, family, parents, teachers, girl friends. Guys didn't want me around, either.

I was a 'yes man.' If somebody was talking about something, I'd agree with them, no matter what. I wanted them to accept me. People really caught on to that. All that put me into my cycle, and I started offending."

STACE
"Growing up, I was constantly abused by my parents in every single form in the world. I didn't go to school. My mom didn't want me to. She was afraid that I'd tell, which is what I eventually did.

My whole life I was taught that sex is how you show your love, your anger, anything. It was the way you showed your feelings.

I thought I was a punching bag, or a sexual pleasure object. I never thought of myself as a person. I thought there was something wrong with me, that I was no good and responsible for everything that happened to me."

KYLE
"My parents got divorced when I was 6. My mom wasn't around much. I missed

my dad. He was out doing a lot of heavy partying and I seldom saw him.

My mom was an alcoholic, out at the bar every night. I felt that she didn't care about me, so I'd do things to get her to notice me.

First I tried setting fires. I got caught, got in trouble, got grounded for a month. That was that. Then I went to offending. I got away with it. I was 9 years old. I just kept on going."

These offenders don't blame their past for their sex-offending behavior. They don't use their past to excuse their offenses. But looking at their past helps them see the roots of feelings and behaviors that became part of their abuse cycle. Just understanding where some of your attitudes and behavior came from doesn't change them, but it can be a tool for helping you to change them.

Questions:

At what age did you first offend?

Do you remember what was going on at home? At school?

How did you feel about yourself back then? Did you have friends? Did you spend a lot of time alone? Did you hang out with younger kids?

What has your relationship with your father/mother or parents been like? Do you feel they were there for you?

Do you think having problems at home and offending is related? Why?

> *Word to Remember:*
>
> **Learned**

Chapter 30: Brothers and Sisters

"She's my little sister. I'm her big brother. I'm supposed to stick up for her. I can't be that anymore. I've lost that."

You may have offended kids who were a lot younger than you are. Even if you didn't, you probably have restrictions on being around younger kids. For instance, maybe you can't be around younger kids unless an adult is present.

You may have offended your younger brother or sister. If you did, maybe you had to move out of your house so that you wouldn't abuse your brother or sister again. You may be angry about having to move, or maybe you miss your family.

When you offend anyone who has trusted you, it hurts that person a lot. The abuse itself may have been physically painful. Your victim also feels **betrayed** by you.

Betrayal is when you act as if you like someone, get them to trust you, then do something to hurt them. **Betrayal** is very painful, but it's not a physical pain. It's like being punched in your feelings. **Betrayal** can take a long time to heal. Sometimes it never

does heal. **Betrayal** is especially painful to younger people.

Most of the time, younger kids look up to their older brothers and sisters. They trust them, and love them a lot, no matter how much they fight with each other. Offending breaks that bond of trust. It's a **betrayal** of trust and love. Sometimes it can't be fixed. Sometimes it can, but it will take a lot of work.

These offenders sexually offended their younger sister or brother. This is what they have to say about how the abuse affected their relationship.

BEN *"I won't be able to have a brother/sister relationship with my sister again. I might be able to talk to her someday, but we won't be close. She can't trust me.*

I shouldn't have done that to her. She's my little sister and I'm her big brother. I'm supposed to stick up for her. I can't be her big brother anymore. I've lost that."

PAUL *"I used to teach my brother wrestling moves all the time. Since I got caught, we don't do that anymore. Part of it has to do with us getting older. But I also think it's because he's afraid something's going to happen. We still talk, but we don't really do anything together anymore."*

DEL *"I used to do a lot of things with my sister – go to the arcade, to the store, things like that. I was her big brother and she looked up to me. I* *didn't have to intimidate her – she just did what I wanted because I was her brother."*

KYLE
"I've talked with my sister a few times on the phone. (I told group about it.) She was angry at me for a long time, but now she wants to see me.

We don't talk about what happened. We just talk about how things are going at school. I like talking to her. I don't even remember what she looks like, it's been so long."

MONTE
"Things have gotten a lot better with my sister. Right after the abuse, she wouldn't acknowledge that I was even related to her. Now, a year later, she's to the point where she wants to see me."

Sometimes a brother or sister doesn't want to believe you're an offender. They are loyal to you. They don't want to see you be in trouble or upset. The way they are loyal is to deny what you've done.

Or because of how you groomed your brother or sister, they think that if you did something wrong, then they must be wrong or in trouble, too. By denying what you did, they are trying not to feel guilty and ashamed.

It's good to have brothers or sisters who love you, but it's not good to let them stay in denial. If this happens in your family, you might want to talk about it with your counselor or in group. It's also very important that your victim know that what you did was not their fault.

YVONNE
"At first my brother tried to minimize what I did. He kept saying the justice system was making up charges. Now he still doesn't know the whole story, but he's accepted what happened. He keeps trying to tell me I can have my record cleared, but with this type of crime, it never goes away. It's always there."

ADAM
"My sisters minimized what I did. They said it wasn't that bad – not as bad as you see on radio or TV. My mom and my friends, too. They said, 'He's not that bad of a person. He shouldn't be up there (locked up).' "

PAUL
"My brother still denies it. He thinks I was charged with something I didn't do. I think he denied it so it wouldn't make me look bad. But if I were to tell him what I did, I think he would be supportive of my treatment."

Here is part of an interview with a young teen who was raped by her brother. You may get a better understanding of her feelings if she speaks in her own words.

Could you talk about what happened to you?

I was 12 when I was raped the first time, 13 the second time. The second time it was my brother. It's hard to turn in your brother to the police, but I did. I was having nightmares, was very depressed. I was in shock and denial. It's one of those things you just don't want to remember....

How did you feel right after your offenses happened?

I felt my body had been betrayed, like I'd been burglarized, violated.

After the first rape, I would take 3 showers a day for about 2 months. It helped me feel cleaner. With my brother, I only did that for about a week.

I felt ugly and disgusting. I had terrible self-esteem. I started doing crappy in school. I couldn't concentrate at all.

What was the hardest thing for you to "get" in your counseling?

That the rapes weren't my fault. At first, I thought they were. I know now most rape victims feel that way. Now I know they weren't. The other thing was that it was my brother who raped me. We had been pretty close and I was very confused.

My counselor helped me realize that loving my brother wasn't wrong, I could just hate what he did. Now I know he has a problem. He needs to learn how to control his sex drive.

How did your family respond when you told them what happened?

My mom thought I did a good thing. But my aunt hated me. She blamed me for turning him in. She said I was just trying to get him out of the house.

At first I felt I was responsible for my brother getting arrested, too. I ran outside when he got taken away in the police car. He was crying. I felt horrible. But I know it was the right thing to do. I turned him in so he would get help and

wouldn't do it to anyone else, ever. I really miss my brother.

Have you been pressured to forgive or not forgive your offenders?

Some of my friends thought I shouldn't forgive my brother. But I love him and I did. It took a couple of months. I never forgave the first guy. There wasn't any pressure to forgive him. I'm still angry at him.

And what about your brother?

He just successfully completed his sex offender program. I'm so proud of him. He called and told me he loved me and that he'd be home soon. He also said there were a few more things he wanted to say to me.

Has he apologized?

I got a couple of letters from him saying what happened was all his responsibility. He told me he misses the good times and the bad times. He wishes he could be with us during the holidays. Maybe some day he will be.

Questions:

Did you offend your brother or sister?

If you did, has it affected your relationship? Do you think it will? How?

Did you have to leave your home because of offending a sibling? What did that feel like?

Have you ever been betrayed by someone you trusted? How did that feel?

Have you been offended by a brother, sister or relative? How did that make you feel?

Do you think Paul's wrestling with his younger brother might have been grooming?

Did you notice any thinking errors in the offenders' comments? Which ones?

Word to Remember:

Betrayal

Chapter 31:
Parents Speak Up

In this chapter we're going to let parents say how they felt when they found out their child was a sex offender. We hope some of what they say will be helpful to you. In the interviews, F means father; M means mother.

Interview #1:
The Masons, Parents of Eli, an adolescent male sex offender.

How did you react when you learned your son had committed sexual offenses?

F: I was totally speechless. I don't think I could speak for a day.

M: I'm his step-mother. I was surprised, shocked. We had always described him as "our perfect child." We were totally taken off guard.

F: We immediately started to minimize it. We said, "It isn't really this bad. It's somebody else's fault."

M: Eli assured us he had just one victim, and that nothing had happened in our home. And we believed him – we didn't have any reason not to. He was always such a good kid. But later we found out he was lying to us.

How did this situation change your family life?

F: At first we minimized the whole situation—that it really wasn't a big deal, that we could handle it ourselves. We believed him when he said he only had one victim, and she wasn't in our family.

But once he told us he had offended his step-sister at our home, everything changed. He had to move out of the house, and he couldn't come visit while his step-sisters were here.

M: I felt so betrayed by him. Eli had lied so much to us by then that I couldn't believe anything he said. I felt like I didn't even know who he was.

F: We had always been one big family. Now he couldn't even be left alone with his brother. It totally disrupted our family life, our holidays. Plus, it's affected other relationships. Eli's's grandparents think he's been treated too harshly by the system and by us. They think we're making too big a deal out of this.

M: I remember going to some classes where they explained what would happen during Eli's treatment. I can remember feeling, "I don't belong here. Our family's too good for this. What are we doing in this icky juvenile detention center?" Now I know that that was real "I'm unique" type of thinking.

Did Eli's offending affect your relationship with him?

F: For M, it's been really difficult. She gets fed up with him, angry, doesn't want anything to do with him anymore. I feel compassion, concern and care for him. That hasn't really changed. I trust him now, but I also don't want to open the door for him to fail again.

M: I feel that I can never really trust him again. When someone lies to you so much, and you feel such betrayal, you can't ever get that total trust back.

Did Eli ever act out sexually in the past, but you didn't see it?

F: Yes. He was 11. My daughter was 5. She came to us and said, 'Eli kissed me. Really hard.' She was upset. We didn't think much of it, just told him not to do it again.

Come to find out, years later, that he had actually molested her. We thought that she had told us everything. Back then, when our reaction was so mild, Eli figured we were saying, 'no big deal.'

I've beat myself up about that reaction. I go, "Why didn't I think to say, 'Is that all that happened?'" But you just don't think to say that. You don't for a second think that your child is a sex offender.

What is the most helpful thing Eli has done to heal the family?

F: He's really been working hard in his treatment. For a while he was not doing his homework, not participating fully. But lately he's been getting stuff done. He's stuck with the program even after he graduated from high school. I've also seen a change in his attitude. He really seems to care more about how other people feel.

M: Eli's much more open and honest now. He's willing to sit down and actually listen to me. He's learning to take responsibility for himself. We decided that our family wasn't going to pay for what Eli did. He has had to get a job and he's paid for everything – for his

counseling, family counseling, phone calls, gas, polygraphs. Everything.

How else has this affected your life?

M: I don't trust anybody. I can't stand to let my kids go places without me. My daughter is becoming a teenager. I know I have to let her do things, but I feel sick whenever she's out and about with her friends.

Also, it changes your way of looking at life. Now I see things – potentially risky things – in other families that other parents don't see.

F: We had been working really hard to get Eli to come home and live with us. The most wrenching thing for me was when our daughter finally told us she would never live in a home with Eli, that if we asked her to, she would move out. I had to tell her that we would never move her out. I had to face that Eli would never again live in our life.

What would your advice be to other parents of sex offenders?

F: Be prepared to learn more and more and more. Don't accuse your child of lying to you. It's so hard for that information to come out. It trickles out very slowly. You think he's lying to you, but it's just that it's so hard to share that information.

M: There's so much pain. You just don't want to know anymore. It hurts so much. The other thing I'd say is, don't trust anyone. It could be the least likely person you'd expect. Oftentimes, those are the kids that hide it the best.

F: You feel it's the strong-willed child you have to battle with all the time. But watch out. The compliant child is the one who could end up being the problem.

Questions:

Did anything the Masons said sound familiar to you? Did your mom and/or dad have feelings like theirs?

Is the way Eli's parents reacted different from the way your parents reacted when they found out about your offending?

Do you think parents should be upset when they find out their child is a sex offender?

Do you think it's fair that Eli has to pay for all of his treatment? Why or why not?

Interview #2:
Tom – Father of Kyle, an adolescent male sex offender.

How did you react when you learned that Kyle had sexually offended?

I was real sick to my stomach. I didn't want to talk to him. I was disappointed in him, and because I was out gettin' drunk all the time, I was ashamed of myself.

For most of the time Kyle was growing up, I wasn't there for him. I lived near him, but I never played with him or took him anywhere. I was only into drinkin' and doin' drugs.

When Kyle was 15 he started drinkin' with me. That was the only way he could get close to me. When he got caught, he came and lived with me, but I didn't stop drinking. I was drunk all the time.

After I got my second drunk driving ticket, I went into treatment. I started realizing how I had never been around for Kyle, never did anything with him or gave him any affection.

I think me not being there had something to do with him offending. He was reaching out for affection, but in the wrong way.

How did Kyle's offending change your family life?

Between Kyle and I and my daughter, we've pulled together. But with the family in general – my sisters, my nieces – there's nothing. His aunts never want to see him again.

My girlfriend lives with me and has a 7-year-old son. We had to make all new rules: No hugging. No sitting on laps. No wrestling around. They couldn't be alone together.

I watch Kyle all the time. If he and I go to town, I watch him out of my side vision. I watch to see if he turns to look at any kids. Any indication that he might be slippin' again, I check him on it or I call up his counselor.

My daughter was offended by Kyle. My ex-wife says our daughter's strong, that she can get through it. But she can't. She's smoking cigarettes, starting to hang with the wrong crowd. Her grades have gone down. She's 13.

Has Kyle being in treatment changed your relationship with him?

We're getting back to a father-and-son relationship. But some things are hard. I read all his homework and I know everything he's done. Some of it sticks in my brain. Sometimes I want to push him back, keep him from getting too close to me. I have to remind myself, 'He's trying. He's doing better.'

It's also made me grow up. What he wrote in his homework was that he did what he did for attention, 'cause he wasn't getting attention from me or his mother. He knew I wasn't there for him.

I've changed my life 180 degrees since this happened.

What's the most helpful thing Kyle's done to heal your relationship?

Sticking with his treatment. At first, Kyle didn't want to do his treatment. I had to really get after him. When he wouldn't do his treatment, I'd get into these mood swings. I was in AA and I was out of work because I got hurt on the job. After 7 months, I had a relapse.

What happened after your relapse?

Actually, things got better. I told my sponsor what was going on, and now I have someone to talk to. And I learned to accept that Kyle really was an offender. And that he was doing something about it. Now things are better. I trust him more. I'm giving him more responsibility, letting him make his own decisions.

What else was difficult for you during his treatment?

I read all his homework. Some of it made me real sick to my stomach. I wanted to beat him, but I knew it wouldn't do any good. It's hard even today to give him a hug. When he got his diploma, he was really proud of it. It was hard to give him a hug at first. I went ahead and did it.

What advice would you give to parents of teenage sex offenders?

Go into this with an open mind. Listen to what's being said. In the beginning, I saw this one counselor. He had long hair, looked strange. The first thing that popped into my mind was, "This guy smokes pot. How's he gonna help my kid?" But after a few meetings with him I found out that I could trust him. I relaxed a lot after that.

What about to parents in general?

Be more involved in your kids' life. Don't take 'em for granted. If you don't, you won't know anything. Happens all the time. A lot of kids are in the same jam Kyle is – parents not giving the kid what he needs.

Questions:

Do you think Tom is a supportive
parent? Why or why not?

Do you think Tom's drinking made him a
bad father?

How do you think Tom's drinking
contributed to Kyle's offending?

Do you think it's a good idea that Kyle
and Tom go to AA meetings together?
Why or why not?

What has your relationship with your
father/mother been like? Do you feel
they were there for you?

What kinds of things do you need to do
to win back your parent's trust?

Section 9.
Victims

Chapter 32:
Betrayal

"I'd be all buddy-buddy. I'd be their friend, their shoulder to cry on. Then, when the opportunity came, boom."

Many offenders victimize someone who is younger or weaker than they are. Offenders feel safe with younger children. They know younger kids are easy to control – by intimidation, threats or even through the child's loyalty.

Offenders learn how to choose their victims. Often they choose kids who look up to them and trust them. They learn to look for kids who are **vulnerable**. People who are **vulnerable** don't have their guard up. They may be looking for love or approval. Often they are very willing to trust others. While people are vulnerable, they are easy to push around. They are not strong and follow others' suggestions or opinions easily. They may have a hard time sticking up for themselves. Many kids who are **vulnerable** most of the time have low self-esteem.

In the chapter on brothers and sisters we talked about **betrayal**. When you hurt someone who trusts you, you **betray** that person. All of the offenders speaking here betrayed their victims. Some of them used **intimidation** to keep their victims from telling. **Intimidation** means you make someone think you will hurt them or get them in serious trouble if they don't do what you want them to do.

Do you remember what **grooming** means? That's when you choose a potential victim, pay them a lot of attention and start getting control over them. **Grooming tactics** are the actual things you do to get the person to trust or like you. You might give them rides on your bike, say nice things to them, take them to play video games or give them candy or ice cream.

JAY *"All my victims were female and **vulnerable**. They were girls who wanted real bad to be accepted. I'd treat 'em real nice, and act like I was accepting them. Then I'd offend them."*

"I'd always choose people who had been offended before. Somehow I always knew. I'd think, 'She's already got low self-esteem. She's gonna trust me, gonna look for acceptance.'

ERIC *"I'd be all buddy-buddy. I'd be their friend, their shoulder to cry on. Then, when the opportunity came, boom."*

PAUL *"My victim looked up to me. She was 6 years younger than me. We had a pretty good relationship. After I offended her, I threatened her. I told her if she told, I'd beat the crap out of her. She was really scared of me, because I was so much bigger than her."*

BARRY *"I had victims that were family members, next-door neighbors, ex-girlfriend's brother and sisters. I looked for kids between 9 and 11. I knew I could get power over them.*

I used a lot of grooming tactics. I'd pay them a lot of attention. Sometimes I'd give my victims candy or toys.

Most of my victims are female. I became like a father figure toward them, or a big brother figure. I got their trust, then I offended them."

Many sex offenders betray others because they've been betrayed themselves. These offenders have stuffed the painful feelings they had when they were betrayed, so they act as if betraying someone else is no big deal.

Well, betraying someone *is* a big deal, whether the person is a member of your family, a neighbor, yourself or a stranger. Can you remember any time you were betrayed? Have you ever betrayed anyone? If you have been betrayed, you can begin to heal that wound instead of passing that pain on by abusing and betraying others.

Questions:

Have you ever been betrayed by someone you trusted? How did it feel?

What do you think that person was thinking about when he or she betrayed you?

What's the difference between pain that's in your body, and pain that's in your heart?

Did you offend someone who trusted you? How do you think that made them feel?

Words to remember:

Intimidate

Vulnerable

Betray

Grooming tactics

Chapter 33: Empathy

"My thinking now is, my victims are the same as me. What if someone offended me? How would I feel? I'm just as vulnerable as they are."

We've talked about **empathy** before, but now we're going to talk about it more because it's so important. **Empathy** is about feeling what someone else is feeling. When someone says what happened to them, you understand in your heart and with your emotions how they might feel.

Many offenders are able to hurt others because they have shut off their own **vulnerable** feelings. **Vulnerable** means you don't feel strong. You feel like someone could easily take control of you. **Vulnerable** feelings include being scared, sad, depressed, hurt or ashamed.

Offenders often "**stuff**" their vulnerable feelings. **Stuffing** feelings means they decide not to feel those feelings, they bury them deep inside. If they are sad, they stuff it. If they are hurt, they stuff it. The only feeling they sometimes don't stuff is anger.

After a while, offenders start to believe they don't have feelings. Then they start to treat other people as if they didn't have feelings, either. It is a lot easier to hurt other people if you believe that you can't feel hurt yourself.

In treatment, you learn to uncover all the feelings you have buried. You start to feel emotions like sadness, disappointment, loneliness, embarrassment and shame. Feeling those feelings isn't pleasant. But being able to know what those feelings are will free you up to really feel other emotions, such as joy, satisfaction and excitement.

Once you understand your own feelings, you can begin to understand other people's feelings. You will begin to understand how your victims felt when you hurt them. That's called learning **empathy**.

Empathy means that you can identify with someone else's feelings. If you have empathy for someone who is feeling sad, that means you feel their sadness.

If offenders had empathy, they would know how much they hurt their victims. Most sex offenders have to struggle to learn empathy. Cutting off empathy is a thinking error and keeps you in your cycle.

BEN *"Empathy for my victim was one of the hardest things for me to 'get.' After I had offended her for awhile, I just didn't think about her feelings anymore. She became an object."*

ELI *"I never gave a thought about how anybody else felt. I was* just worried about myself. I had a real lack of empathy.

Learning empathy takes a long time. First, you have to know what your own feelings are. If you can't feel your own feelings, then you can't feel anyone else's either."

MONTE
"One of the things that's helped me understand empathy has been role-playing, when I play the victim and somebody else is the offender. It makes me feel really small. I really get the image of how my victims must have felt."

BARRY
"I've been dealing with my victimization, and it helps. If you can remember how you felt when you were victimized, you can think, 'I don't want somebody else to go through what I went through.' That kind of helps you not victimize someone else."

Learning to have empathy won't happen quickly. If you keep being honest about your own vulnerable feelings, you will learn empathy. Having empathy will help make you not want to re-offend anyone, ever.

Having empathy will also make your relationships with people better. You will be able to talk to people about things that matter to you and the other person. You will have better relationships with other people. That will be a very satisfying feeling.

Questions:

What does being vulnerable feel like to you?

How do you act when you're feeling vulnerable?

Explain what empathy means.

How do you think your victims felt when you offended them?

Did you think about your victims' feelings before you offended them? After?

Why is it important to have empathy for other people?

Words to Remember:

Empathy

Victimization

Vulnerable

Stuffing feelings

Chapter 34:
Excuses

"I told myself, kids this young don't have feelings."

Remember what **thinking errors** are? Thinking errors are mental tricks you play on yourself. They allow you to think that abusive or dishonest behavior is OK.

Offenders have to make up reasons why it's OK to offend. Those reasons are called "excuses." They use thinking errors to make excuses for having sexually assaulted someone else.

Can you spot the thinking errors in these statements? (Remember, a list of thinking errors is in the Appendix.)

BEN *"I told family members my sister was flirting with me, that she wanted me to. I made it sound like it was all her fault.*

I thought I could just do anything I wanted to my victims. Get my needs met. Put myself first, make myself feel better."

STACE *"I said to myself, 'Sex is what my mom taught me and that's what I should teach him.' He was going to be my half-brother, so I figured, 'He needs to know how to love people.'*

And to me, abusing someone was love. Even though I knew he didn't want it."

ERIC *"With guys, if I'd touch them or something, I'd make it look like an accident. I'd turn around and say, 'Joke.' That way I knew they weren't going to say nothin'. Or I'd think, 'If you can get 'em to trust you, you can talk 'em into it.'"*

DEL *"I chose my victims by how smart they were, and their size. I chose kids who were slow, so they didn't catch on to what I was doing. I made it seem that they wanted it too."*

YVONNE *"I said, 'It's OK. It's normal. People do it everyday.' He had power, and I didn't, and I wanted his power. I wanted control, so I took it. Just like that."*

PAUL *"I told myself, 'It was OK. I won't get in trouble for this. Nothing's going to happen. It's not really against the law.'"*

ELI *"I would sneak into my victims' rooms. I thought, 'They won't know, and what they don't know won't hurt 'em.' Sometimes they were awake. I just figured their embarrassment would keep 'em from telling."*

MONTE *"In order to offend, I would make myself into an emotionless, feelingless person. That way, without any emotions, I could offend."*

BARRY

"I'd tell myself: 'They're young, they don't know what I'm doing. They don't know that what I'm doing is wrong. At their age, they don't have feelings.'"

Did any of these excuses make sense to you? Did any of them sound familiar? Can you see how these offenders used mental tricks to convince themselves that sexually assaulting someone else was OK behavior?

Sex offenders aren't the only people who use excuses. Almost everybody uses excuses at one point or another. The difference is that sex offenders use excuses to make behavior that hurts someone else seem OK. In treatment, you will get to know the excuses you used to make your offending behavior seem OK. Soon you will be able to tell right off when other offenders are using excuses, too.

Questions:

What did you tell yourself to make your offending seem "OK?"

What thinking errors did you use that gave you "permission" to hurt your victims?

What do you think the person you abused would think about your excuses?

How can you tell when other offenders in the group are making up excuses?

Word to remember:

Thinking errors

Chapter 35:
Changing Your Attitude

"I think now before I act. I look at how I'd feel if that happened to me – getting called names or being hurt."

In treatment, you will learn to understand and respect your feelings. You will also start to understand other people's feelings. You will begin to see how badly you hurt your victims. This won't be easy, especially at first.

Many things may help you change the way you treat other people. You may relate to the pain other kids in your group feel from their past. You may begin to feel less alone in your own feelings. Maybe you will begin to understand the pain your victims felt when you hurt them.

These offenders feel very differently about their victims since being in treatment. They feel differently towards other people in general. Can you see how they have changed their attitudes?

KYLE *"I see my victims as people now, hurt people. I want to make it up to them. I want to apologize for what I've done, but I know there isn't any way I can."*

JAY *"I think that what I did was really bad. I hurt all my victims. My thinking now is, they're just like me. I'm just as vulnerable as they are. And what if somebody raped me? It's really hard for me to say this, but I really believe it."*

ALEXIS *"I have a lot more feelings toward my brothers and sisters now. When I was offending I wasn't even thinking about them, just about what I wanted. I care about them more now."*

ERIC *"I'm really sorry for what I did. I feel like I messed up my victims' lives. Maybe I created someone exactly like me, who will go on to offend someone else.*

Now they have this low self-esteem, and the things that go with being offended: the insecurity about yourself, your sexuality."

DEL *"Before, I didn't have empathy for any of my victims. Now I do. Before, I didn't care if my victims got help. Now I want every one of them to get help."*

BARRY *"I used to think all of my victims were mean, that they didn't have any feelings. That they didn't care about anybody.*

Now I know they have really hurt feelings, and they'll have to live with what I did for the rest of their lives. I know how I felt when I was victimized. I can understand those feelings of betrayal."

In treatment you will get to know yourself better. You will also start to look at other people differently, too. It won't be easy to accept how much you have hurt people by sexually abusing them. Part of treatment – and part of growing up – is accepting the mistakes you have made, without minimizing them and without running from them. This will be a hard but important step in your treatment.

Questions:

Do you believe these offenders are truly sorry for the pain they have caused their victims?

Has your attitude towards your victims changed since you've been in treatment? What did it used to be? What is it now?

What made you change your attitude?

If you could talk to each of your victims, what would you tell him or her?

Has your attitude toward other people changed? How?

Chapter 36:
Offenders Can Be Victims, Too

"Here was somebody I looked up to and trusted – my cousin. I thought what he was doing must be OK. But it didn't feel OK."

Many sex offenders are also victims of sexual abuse, but not all. For many of them, that is how they have learned to abuse others. Many offenders have buried memories of their abuse, because they don't want to remember that it happened.

Being a victim of sexual abuse is not an excuse for offending other people. Most people who are sexually abused don't react by offending other people, but some do. Most people who are sexually abused have low self-esteem because of the abuse. For some, that low self-esteem can be the beginning of an offending cycle.

Victims can be male or female, just as offenders can be male or female. Males in our society usually don't talk about being sexually abused. It's just not considered a manly thing to do, or a guy may worry that people will think he's gay if he talks about being sexually abused by a man. Because few guys talk about it, many

males who have been abused think they are the only ones this has happened to. That isn't true. Most of the sex offenders we know about are male, and many of them have same-sex victims. That means a lot of males have been the victims of sexual abuse by men or older boys.

Women also sexually abuse kids. When female offenders were abused by a woman or an older girl, it's also pretty hard to talk about. And boys who are offended by women think they're supposed to enjoy it, that it's not really abuse. If they tell anyone, they may be congratulated for "scoring" at a young age, or told how lucky they were to have an experienced teacher.

Most of the offenders in this book didn't even think about their victimization until they were in counseling. Some of them think being a victim had a big effect on them, some of them don't.

Here some of them talk about how their abuse has affected them.

ADAM *"I didn't know what my father did was an offense until he got arrested for it. My mom asked me if I knew it was sex abuse. I told her no ... Being abused by him wasn't a big part of why I offended."*

BARRY *"When I was 9, my cousin offended me. He used me as an object. He was 13 and he was a father figure to me, 'cause my dad wasn't around.*

I totally blocked what he did out of my mind. I swore up and down at the first treatment center that I had never been offended.

But then people started talking about how they were offended, and it brought back memories. Then I came here, and we had to write our sexual history. It came out that I had been victimized by 6 or 7 different people."

MONTE *"I was offended when I was*
younger. I didn't know what was going on. I thought it was a big joke, a game. The person who offended me was 16; I was 10.

I think it gave me a distorted image of what sex was supposed to be. It didn't play a big role in my offending, but it played a part."

YVONNE *"Being victim-*
ized traumatizes you so much. You lose so much of your power, you just want to get it back. If you can't get it by being a regular kid, you're going to get it by the way you were victimized."

Being sexually abused can be very confusing. Some parts may feel good, and some parts feel terrible. If you are male, and were offended by an older female, it can be even more confusing. Most people don't think females can be sex offenders. If you say anything, people may not believe you. Or they may say, "That wasn't abuse at all. You were lucky!"

That is not true. If you've been touched sexually by a female two or more years older

than you, you weren't "lucky." You were abused. It doesn't make any difference if you said OK, if you asked, or if you felt some pleasure. It is still abuse. It is abuse because of the misuse of power.

The same thing holds true for girls who were abused by other females. Many people don't believe that females abuse other females, but it happens. It's very important to tell your counselor or group if this has happened to you, even if it happened when you were very young.

Here some offenders talk about how they felt about being offended by a female.

JAY *"When I was 14, 15, I was having sex with older*
women who were 20, 25. I felt accepted. They were mother figures to me, 'cause I didn't really have a mom. Now I think I was being used.

I told some people about it, but they said it wasn't any big deal. All you hear in the papers is about men offending women or younger kids. You never hear about women harassing or raping.

It was pretty confusing. I kept thinking, 'why do they want me?' "

BEN *"I was offended by a female when I was 8. I*
asked her to. She was five years older than me. Then, I didn't really feel violated. I wasn't old enough to understand that was really abuse, too.

But if it had been done by a male, it would have been totally different. I would have been disgusted. I'm not bisexual. I don't want to be offended by a guy. I'd really feel violated if it was done by a male."

BARRY *"I was abused by females*

twice. I always thought it was consensual, but they were 4-6 years older than I was.

I was confused, because there was some pleasure. We talked about that in group. Even though you're a victim, your body likes to be touched. It's like someone has you pinned and they're tickling you. You're body's laughing, but you're hurting inside. It's the same kind of thing."

As you go further into treatment, you may remember abuse that happened a long time ago. You may discover that things you never thought were abuse, actually were. You may uncover abuse that happened to you when you were very young.

When you start to understand how deeply sexual abuse has affected you, or others in your group, you will better understand how deeply you hurt your victims when you abused them. All of us have a sexuality. It is very sensitive and very powerful. When it is disturbed, our whole lives are disturbed.

Questions:

Has someone two or more years older than you or more powerful than you ever touched you sexually – on your genitals? (Genitals are sexual parts of your body. For males that means the penis, testicles, buttocks and anus. For females it means their breasts, vagina, anus and buttocks.) This can also include being kissed in a sexual way, or on any of your sexual parts. It also includes having someone ask you to kiss or touch them in a sexual way.

If this has happened, did you know at that time that this behavior was sexual abuse? How did you feel when this happened?

Did you feel that something was wrong? Did you understand that the abuser was the one doing something wrong, not you?

When a male sexually touches a much younger female or in a situation where the male is misusing his power to get sex, it is called abuse. Often, when an older female touches a younger male or female, people don't call it abuse. Why do you think this is true? What do you think about this difference?

Chapter 37:
Offenders as Victims:
Same-sex Abuse

"I knew what he did was wrong, but I felt I had to pay him back for what he'd given me."

A big reason males don't tell when they are abused by another male is that they are afraid people will think they are **homosexual**. Or they may think that having that experience will make them homosexual. Girls who are offended by other females often feel the same way. Girls may also feel like no one will believe them because people hear much less about female sex abusers.

Being abused by a person of your gender doesn't make you a homosexual. Even if you felt some pleasure when the abuse happened, it still doesn't mean you are a homosexual. The body can feel pleasure when it is touched in certain ways, and it doesn't necessarily care about the gender of the person doing the touching.

Being abused by a same-sex offender becomes a big deal when the victims become afraid that means they are homosexual or "**gay**." Being gay is something they fear because gay people

are treated badly by many people in our society.

Some males who have had same-sex abusers may try hard to prove to themselves and others that they are not homosexual. They may act super tough, or macho. They may talk about sex a lot, or try to get lots of females to be sexual with them. They may show great dislike of homosexuals in general (the word for that is **homophobia**). Females who have had same-sex abusers may want sexual contact with males just to prove to themselves that they aren't homosexual (female homosexuals are called **lesbians**).

If you have offended people of your gender it doesn't mean you are a homosexual, either. Many offenders in this book have victims of both genders. Sexually abusing someone is first of all about having power over that person. For many sex abusers, the gender of their victim is not the most important part of the abuse.

Many people now believe that being homosexual is something a person is born with, not something that happens as a result of abuse or bad parenting. Other people believe **sexual orientation** is determined by a number of different factors.

There is nothing wrong with you if you have sexual feelings for persons of your same sex. Sexual feelings or behavior between people of the same age and power can be normal for them. Sexual feelings only become "wrong" when they are acted upon inappropriately, regardless of whether it is a same-sex or heterosexual situation.

If you have had a same-sex offender, it's very important to talk about that in treatment. You may not be aware of how much this abuse has affected you. Talking about it may help you understand some of your behaviors and attitudes.

Some of the offenders in this book have been sexually abused by someone of their gender.

Here they talk about how that affected them.

DEL *"I was offended when I was 5 and when I was 12. The second time my offender coaxed me, took me for rides on his motorcycle, gave me cigarettes, stuff like that. I knew what he did was wrong, but I felt I had to pay him back for what he'd given me. I learned everything from him – how to groom, stuff like that. He was 17.*

I was confused because I had felt some pleasure with him. I was afraid I was gay. Now I know that having sex with a male doesn't mean you are gay. I know I'm not gay now, but before I went through treatment I was afraid I was."

ERIC *"I was offended when I was 9, 10 and 12. By my cousin – a guy – and two others. Each time I felt sick, dirty, confused. I didn't tell anybody until I got into treatment. Then I only told what happened when I was 9. One of the reasons I didn't tell was that I didn't want people to think I was gay."*

STACE *"I was only abused by my mother, not my dad. My biggest fear from that was that I was going to grow up gay. It*

scared me to death. I didn't talk to anyone about that. I didn't want no one to know."

Our sexual identity is at the core of who we are as individuals. That's one reason why sexually abusing someone hurts them so deeply. It's also why you shouldn't bury or hide the confusion you might have about your sexual identity. There are many ways to be a healthy sexual person. Your counselor or group leader can help you see this. They can help you sort out your true feelings from your fears.

Questions:

Have you experienced same-sex abuse as a victim? If you have:

Has it made you think you might be a homosexual?

How do you think it has affected your self-image or your behavior?

Have you offended someone of your same sex? Has it made you think or fear you may be homosexual?

If any of these questions apply to you, have you talked to anyone about your fears? Why or why not?

Do you have strong feelings about homosexuality? What are they?

Words to Remember:

Homosexual

Homophobia

Gay

Lesbian

Sexual Orientation

Chapter 38:
Survivors of Abuse
Speak Out

In this section are short interviews with two survivors of abuse. They will tell you what being offended was like for them, and how it has affected their lives.

Seventeen-year-old **Karin** was offended by her father for a number of years. They have both been through treatment.

Karin

What was the hardest thing for you to get through your head when you were in counseling?

That it wasn't my fault. There's just something inside every victim that says it's your fault, that you could have fought harder, dressed different, there were things you could have done.

But you learn to tell yourself it wasn't your fault. It takes a long time, but you learn to believe it.

It took a long time for me to get down to the root of how I was feeling. The root was hurt, and being neglected by my mom and used by my dad.

What feeling were you walking around with in your every day life?

That it didn't happen.

How do you think this abuse has affected your life? Has it affected your ability to trust people?

Yeah. I get real jumpy and nervous if I'm alone with an older man. It's also affected my trust with guys my own age. It's really hard for me to make new friends. I'm not really that open.

What makes you think you can trust someone?

People who are really talkative and honest. People with the same beliefs as I have. Then I know I have some sort of common ground.

Has your abuse affected your body image?

Yes. I wear my coat all the time. I never take showers after PE. I'd rather go around stinking than take a shower around other people. I won't expose myself like that.

Sometimes I try to change my weight by not eating. Then I eat a lot. Then I get mad at myself. Then I don't eat. On the one hand, I want to look good. But on the other hand I don't want to attract the wrong type of people.

Have you learned to set limits in your relationships with guys?

Before I didn't. Right now, I'm doing really good in setting my standards and sticking to them.

I have a boyfriend. In the beginning of our relationship, we were sexually active. That hurt the relationship a lot. Now, we've changed. He respects the change, and he's changed along with it.

What does it feel like to have someone accept your limits?

It feels really good. It feels like I'm respected by the other person. Not just an object.

Do you think treatment has changed your dad?

Yeah I do, a lot. He looks at people as people instead of objects, instead of using them. He cares, is more understanding.

A lot of kids who've been abused say, "I just want to be normal. I just want to be like everybody else." Is that possible?

There's no possible way that you could. You're going to have to live with yourself and what happened to you for the rest of your life. You're just going to have to be willing to be the best you can be.

People say that people who get offended are usually the people that offend. And I tell myself, no, I'm never going to do that to my kid. Or that I'm going to look for a guy who does that. And yet, my first true love was really abusive toward me. It was a bad relationship. I find myself scared of who I get involved with.

Sixteen-year-old **Mari** was offended by her mother's boyfriend.

Mari

How did being in counseling help you?

I needed to understand what happened. I didn't even know it was abuse, at first. Not until I talked with my brother's girlfriend. She told me.

My abuse wasn't extreme. It didn't go on for years, and it didn't happen with anyone in my family. But in group I learned it doesn't matter how extreme your abuse was. All abuse hurts somebody in some way.

What was the hardest thing to "get" in your counseling?

That there was a cycle that abusers had. I didn't really understand what those cycles were. When I finally understood, I went, "Oh God, I should have known." My offender would tickle and wrestle with me all the time. Now I know they were steps in his cycle, but I didn't know it back then.

How do you feel toward your abuser?

I never want to see him again.

Have you told your boyfriend what happened?

About ten months ago. He was supportive, but he was kind of scared to hug me after that.

What have you learned to look for in people that you want to date, or be friends with?

If somebody is really gentle, and doesn't always grope you, and likes sitting there talking with you, that's what I like. Somebody who can tell you they care about you without having to show it all the time, like always have to touch you.

Another thing, you have to figure out whether someone is telling the truth or not, that's the main thing. You have to know if the person is trustworthy.

How is your life going now?

I have everything I need right now – a job, friends, a boyfriend, a good place to live. I'm more in touch with people, with what they feel. I understand more things now, and I know how to help people a little bit more. Still I wish it had never happened.

Questions:

Do Karin or Mari say anything that you agree with? If so, what is it?

Do you think Karin's dad is a sex offender? Is Mari's mother's boyfriend a sex offender? Why or why not?

Do you think Karin and Mari are healing from their abuse? What things did they say that make you think that?

Do you think you have changed your victims' lives? How? What feelings do you have about that?

Are your victims getting the help they need to feel better about themselves?

What kind of help do you think your victims need?

Section 10.
Peers

Chapter 39:
What About Making Friends?

"I have a hard time making friends with kids my own age. Most of my friends are younger. I don't know why. Maybe it's because I'm older and they look up to me."

Good friends make life fun. You do stuff together, like laugh, play sports, hang out. You can talk to friends when you are having a hard time. People your own age, or within a year or two are called **peers**.

When you don't have any friends, you can feel bad. You feel "out of it." You can feel that you are not a likeable person.

Making friends with kids their own age is hard for many sex offenders. Most offenders don't have much self-esteem or confidence. They may feel they are worthless, so they don't know how to value others. They are out of touch with their feelings, and so lack empathy for other people's feelings. Having a poor self-image makes it hard to make friends.

Some offenders don't know what a true friend is. They will call someone they hardly know "a friend." Some think the only way to have friends is to have a certain "image." They think that if they were to act like their true self, no one would want to be their friend.

It's embarrassing not to have friends. It's also lonely. Many offenders will start hanging out with younger kids instead of having friends their own age. With younger kids, they feel more in control of the relationship. Some offenders hang out with older kids. In an older crowd they feel less pressure and more acceptance. Sometimes they may be sexually abused by these older "friends," but that's the price of being accepted. They also think it boosts their "image."

See if you can see examples of this in what these offenders say.

MONTE *"I used to have a hard time making friends my own age. I wanted to be around kids who were younger than me. They would look up to me – I was their idol."*

BEN *"I hang out with an older crowd, I get along with them better because they're not so immature."*

BARRY *"I have a hard time making friends with kids my own age. I don't know why. Maybe it's because with younger kids I'm older and they look up to me. They accept me more than people my own age. Even here (in lock-up), most of the people I'm friends with are younger than I am."*

STACE *"I trust people quicker than I did before, but I'm more trusting with males than with females, because I was abused by my mom, not my step-dad."*

JAY *"All my life I've hung around with older people. I've hardly had friends my age. But I get along with these people here (in lock-up). They're around my age."*

PAUL *"I've been able to make friends easy my whole life. It's one of those personality traits I have."*

As you go through treatment, you will find that the types of people you want for friends will change. You will see that you have the right to be seen and appreciated for who you really are, not for your image and not just for sex. You won't need to be seen as a "hero" by younger kids to feel OK about yourself. You won't have to tag along with older kids to feel accepted. You will start looking for friends who can share things with, who are close to you in age and interests.

Questions:

What is a friend?

What's the difference between a friend and an acquaintance?

Are your friends mostly younger than you, the same age, or older than you?

If most of your friends are younger than you, do you know why? What is it you like about having younger friends?

If your friends are mostly older, do you know why? What is it you like about having older friends?

What do you like about having friends the same age as you?

Do you have a hard time making friends? Do you know why?

What could you do to make more friends who are peers?

Words to Remember:

Peers

Self-esteem

Chapter 40:
Should I Tell My Friends About Treatment?

"I think I should tell people. It scares me, but it lets 'em know where I'm at, how I am. I am a sex offender. People shouldn't trust me right off."

If you're just starting treatment, you are probably sure that you will never tell any of your friends about being in treatment. That's OK. You have a lot of other things to think about right now.

After you've been in treatment a while, you may start thinking you want to tell some of your close friends that you are in treatment.

This is a hard decision to make. You want your friends to like you. You want them to stick around. But you also want to be honest with them. Telling them you are a sex offender is scary. Maybe they won't understand. Maybe they won't talk to you anymore. Maybe they'll tell other people, and then no one will want to talk to you, or maybe worse.

On the other hand, maybe your friends will stick by you. They may be shocked at first. But if they are true friends, and if they see that you are taking responsibility for your behavior and doing your treatment, they will probably give you a chance.

Some of the offenders in this book haven't told any of their friends about being in treatment. Some have told only close friends. Here are some of their experiences.

DEL *"In the beginning I lied to my friends about treatment. Now I don't feel a need to lie about it at all. I would tell a good friend."*

BEN *"Some of my friends on the outs know I'm a sex offender. I was afraid to tell 'em. I was afraid it was going to get spread around. But no one who's found out rejected me or anything."*

ALEXIS *"My best friend asked me why I was living with my grandparents. I knew I could trust her. So I just told her. She was quiet, then she said, 'I don't think anything different of you, but I'm kind of surprised.' Sometimes I talk with her about treatment. It's really helpful."*

MONTE *"I've told a few really close friends I felt I could trust. I haven't had a friend – male or female – turn me away after I told them.*

I also think telling my friends is my own form of taking responsibility for what I did.

To let people know who I am. To let people know I'm not the perfect person I used to try and act like."

BARRY *"I told 2 people on the outs –* *my girlfriend at the time and my best friend. They said, 'What happened, happened. That was then, this is a different time. Let's move on.' That helped me a lot."*

PAUL *"I didn't tell any of my* *friends. Some of 'em know I'm on probation, but I told 'em I got into a fight with a younger guy and beat him up.*

I haven't told 'em the truth because I'm afraid I'll lose 'em as a friend. That they won't think as highly of me, won't respect me anymore.

Two guys at school are in group, too. I can trust 'em. If they were to say something about me, I could say it back about them, so I don't think they'll say anything."

ELI *"One person I've told* *everything to. He was surprised, as most people were. Our relationship hasn't changed any."*

ADAM *"Most of my friends* *know now. I told them. It was hard, but I felt they had to know that I'm two people in one. A nice guy on the outside, but at the same time I've done disgusting things to kids. They needed to know that if we were going to keep our relationship."*

The younger you are, the more important it is to be very careful about who you tell about being in treatment. Your circle of friends probably changes a lot these days. You are still learning what real friends are. You are learning about the kinds of people you can trust and those you can't.

You don't want to put yourself in a situation in school or in your neighborhood where you might get hurt. If you are having trouble taking ownership of your sex offending behavior, or are still in denial, it will be even harder for you if there are rumors about you going around your school. This might be a real good topic to talk about in your group or with your counselor.

Being open about something you've always kept secret may seem impossible to you right now. As you learn to take ownership for your abusing, you will be able to let those secrets "out." Your self-confidence will grow and you will develop the courage to be truthful about who you are.

???▶

Questions:

Have told any of your friends you're in treatment? Why or why not?

If you have told friends, what was their reaction?

Do any kids in your school know you have committed sex offenses? If so, what was their reaction?

How do you think your friends would react if they found out from someone else about your being in treatment?

Which type of friends, if any, do you think need to know about your past?

If you told your some of your friends, what kinds of reactions would be helpful and supportive? What kinds would be hurtful and negative?

If some of your friends or classmates reacted negatively, how are you feeling? How are you dealing with these feelings so you don't go into your abuse cycle?

Words to Remember:

On the outs

Taking ownership

Chapter 41:
Girlfriends and Boyfriends

"A girlfriend? I don't see how you could have an honest relationship without telling her."

A few of you may have had romantic relationships with a peer, someone near your own age. Sooner or later, most of you will. Then you'll have to decide if you should tell your girlfriend or boyfriend that you are now in or have been through sex offender treatment. You'll have to decide if it's the best thing to tell them, when to tell them, and how.

Again, there's a lot to be afraid of here. Maybe the person you're seeing will be shocked, and drop you like a hot potato. Maybe he or she will be nice to your face, but little by little start to pull away. Maybe they will tell someone else when they get mad at you.

On the other hand, maybe the person will want to learn more about treatment and how it has helped you. Maybe sharing this information will make you better friends.

There is no rule that says you have to tell your girlfriend or boyfriend that you have been through sex offender treatment. This is especially true if you are in middle school or

the first couple years in high school. Relationships change quickly in those years. You need to go very slow in deciding who to tell about your treatement.

But if you are older, you may get to a point in your relationship with someone where you think you need to share this part of your life with them. They will need to have that information so they can make healthy decisions about your relationship.

Most of the offenders in this book don't have boyfriends or girlfriends now, but they've thought about a time when they might. Here is what they have to say.

JAY *"I don't think I'd tell a girl on the first date. But I'd tell my girlfriend, if we were going to be married. If she really loves me, she'll probably stay. She'll understand."*

ELI *"As far as I'm concerned, I don't plan on telling a girl anything unless I get real close to her. If I decide to marry, I'm definitely going to tell."*

BEN *"I told my girlfriend what I had done, and I felt better, because I wasn't hiding stuff from her. She knew what I did was wrong and sick, but she didn't stop going out with me. After a while I wasn't there for her, so she just broke up with me."*

ALEXIS *"If I get a boyfriend, I'm not going to tell him. Because I think the first thing that would happen is he would* *not want to be around me. Then he'd break up with me."*

PAUL *"I've had a girlfriend for about a month. She doesn't know I'm in treatment. I might tell her later, like a long time later. By that time I'd feel I could trust her enough."*

BARRY *"I'm still in contact with the girl I told. We're not still going out, but we're good friends. She's supportive of me staying in treatment."*

It's hard to know what you're going to do in this kind of situation before you are actually there. But it's important to think about the choices you have. If you are thinking about telling your girlfriend or boyfriend about being in treatment, talk about it to your counselor or group first.

Questions:

If you have a girl/boy friend, have you told him/her about being in treatment? Why or why not?

At what point in a relationship do you think it is important to tell your girl/boy friend about your sex offending behavior?

When would a parent have a right to know? Why?

If the tables were reversed and your girlfriend or boyfriend was in sex offender treatment, would you want to know? If so, when would you want to be told?

If you don't tell your girlfriend or boyfriend that you are a sex offender, and they find out from someone else, how do you think they might react?

What conditions need to be met before a sex offender starts to date?

Why do sex offenders have to be more careful about their dating behavior than non-sex offenders?

If a girlfriend or boyfriend broke up with you when you told them, what would you do to deal with your feelings? How would you keep yourself out of your abuse cycle?

Did you notice any thinking errors in the reasons these offenders gave for telling or not telling?

Chapter 42:
Getting Close to People

"I don't like to set myself up to be hurt. So I just brush people off."

Sometimes the people who act like they don't care if they have friends are the people who actually want them the most. When people feel bad about themselves, they often think other people won't like them. They don't want to be rejected, so they act like they don't really need any friends.

That acting is called having an image. We talked about image in Section 1. Sometimes people will create an image that says, "I don't care if you like me or not." This way they keep people away from them. They think their image will protect them from getting hurt.

In treatment you learn the difference between your image and the real you. Then you get to think about how you will approach other people with the real you. Being real with other people feels pretty different from keeping up an image. It means being honest about your feelings and your goals.

Some offenders find it hard to get close to other teens outside of treatment, some don't. Some offenders have a problem making friends with females, some have a problem making friends with males. Where do you fit in?

BARRY *"With females, it's hard for me to have a relationship of any type. Most of my victims were female. I always think, if I become really close friends with a girl, am I going to want to victimize her? But I can become friends with almost any male."*

STACE *"Being in treatment is not something I keep on my shoulders. I don't wake up thinking about it. Don't go to bed thinking about it. I'm not afraid to get close to people. I'm a lot more trusting than I used to be. I'm around kids all the time, I'm not hurtful. I know I'm not going to do it again."*

PAUL *"I'm really close with a bunch of my friends, we're like brothers and sisters. It's not really hard. It's easier, because for one the drugs aren't there. And my attitude has changed. I'm nicer, so they can get closer.*

Before, I didn't want anyone to get close to me. I thought they would start asking me questions about my past. But I decided to try it, and now I have close friends who accept me."

JAY *"In some ways, it's easier to get close to people because I've been in treatment. I have better social skills since I've been in here. I can talk to* *people appropriately, instead of just talking about sex or drugs."*

MONTE *"It's more difficult to get into a relationship with a person when you're in treatment, because you're still trying to figure out what a proper relationship is.*

But it's easier to become friends with people, too, because in group you learn about people's feelings, about emotion, things like that. You get to understand people better."

Making a new friend is like an adventure. There's a lot to discover. But you don't want to end up in a dead-end gully. Take your time about making friends. It's OK not to trust people right off the bat. Going through treatment will change you, and it will change the types of people you want for friends. You may not know right away who these different friends will be. Take your time. You'll know it when the right people come along.

Questions:

Do you like getting close to people your age? Why, or why not?

Has being in treatment made it easier or harder for you to get close to people? Why do you think that?

If you are in a treatment group, do you feel close to some of the kids in group? Why do you think that is?

Words to Remember:

Image

Being real

Section 11.
Older Offenders
Speak Out

Chapter 43:
Jeff

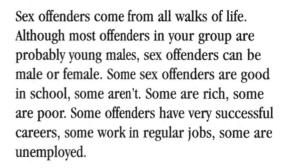

Sex offenders come from all walks of life. Although most offenders in your group are probably young males, sex offenders can be male or female. Some sex offenders are good in school, some aren't. Some are rich, some are poor. Some offenders have very successful careers, some work in regular jobs, some are unemployed.

No matter what their background, the issues offenders have to deal with are the same. They have to:

- Become totally honest about their offending behavior and take full responsibility for all of their offenses.

- Learn about and be willing to change their thinking errors

- Become familiar with their abuse cycle, identify when they are entering their cycle and know how to use tools to get out

- Learn how to stop their inappropriate, deviant and/or hurtful behaviors

- Learn how to interrupt inappropriate or deviant fantasies

- Identify and appropriately express their emotions

- Learn empathy and respect for their victims and other people

- Learn how to live a productive life within society's laws

- Develop self-respect and confidence

Here are some interviews with offenders who didn't get caught until they were older. Think about how their lives may have been different if they had been able to get help when they were younger.

Jeff is in his 60s. He's been an airplane pilot, a journalist and an opera singer. He's even been in movies. But none of these talents helped him deal with his offending behavior. Here he tells how it feels to be sitting on top of the world, and then to fall to the bottom.

How old were you when you first offended?

I'll explain it this way. When I was about 14-17, I was molested – by a Baptist minister's son, a lieutenant in a military training camp, and by my vocal coach. I buried those experiences in my mind and never told anyone. When I was about 30, I bought a boat. My friends, sometimes adults and sometimes teens, would stay overnight on the boat.

That was the first time I had been in close physical contact with teens who were the same age I was when I was victimized. All my offenses happened on that boat. I molested them the same way I was molested.

How did you feel about your offending behavior?

Shame and embarrassment. Every teen I offended was someone who trusted me. It would bother me for days and days. But I didn't want to think about how I was hurting my victims. I thought I would never get caught.

What happened when you were caught?

I was indicted on counts of oral sodomy and first degree sexual abuse. I admitted my guilt, and served 17 months in the county jail. After I got out, I went through treatment.

Before I got caught, I was a very respected member of the community. I was president of a civic club. I spoke at the university. I was a Grand Marshal in parades. I was retired, but I was making a lot of money writing for magazines. I had a wife and wonderful kids.

After I was caught, I lost almost all of it. The story hit the papers, and the wonderful trust that I had from people vanished in the tick of a clock. I had to give up my writing and I lost a lot of money. But the greatest loss was loss of people's trust. I had never, ever, been so low or felt so worthless.

What was the hardest part of treatment for you?

Disclosing to the group. Some of the offenders' wives were there. I didn't want to talk about what I had done in front of them. I felt I was demeaning myself in public.

But talking in front of the group and in front of other groups helped me face the reality of who I was and what I had done.

What thinking errors allowed you to offend your victims?

I never drew the line between adulthood and adolescence. To me, from age 14 on, a boy was an adult. That isn't true.

Why didn't you ever disclose your victimization?

I was afraid. I thought that somehow I was at fault. Now, I know that's not true, but then I didn't.

Did you have a false "image?" What was it?

I was always on stage. I was never really me. I was a phoney. On the outside I acted like I deserved everything I got. But inside, I felt the opposite.

When I got caught, my image disappeared, quicker than putting a pin in a balloon. I felt like the lowest thing on earth. I had absolutely nothing: no character, no reputation, no trust from others, no love, no friendship.

If you not been caught, would you have stopped? If you hadn't gone through treatment?

I would have offended again if I had not been caught. I would have offended to my dying day, if the circumstances were right.

But I also know that if I had been confronted by anybody, I would have stopped. Inside I was begging for treatment, but I didn't have the will

power to ask for it. That would have meant admitting "I'm a sex offender," and I didn't want to do that.

Thank God for the teen who turned me in. I bless him for doing that. He did me the greatest favor in the world.

What do you want to say to younger offenders who are in treatment?

You are a sex offender. Say it openly, and believe it. Otherwise it will be like the worm in the apple that spoils the whole apple. That apple is your life.

You know, I did a lot of things in my life. I was arrested in Cuba. I was held hostage by a crazed gunman. I thought I had lots of courage.

Yet, I was the biggest coward in the world, because I didn't have the guts to go and tell somebody, hey, there's something eating at me that's going to destroy me. That was my offending.

If a person is an offender, it's like herpes. It can go away for a long long time. Then all of a sudden – after 7 or 8 years – it pops up again. Don't kid yourself. If you don't deal with it, it'll happen again.

Jeff's story shows how powerful the urge to abuse someone is. It shows why people with this problem need to get treatment. Jeff had a career, a family and community status, but none of that stopped him from being a sex offender. Even though Jeff was an adult when

this problem need to get treatment. Jeff had a
career, a family and community status, but
none of that stopped him from being a sex
offender. Even though Jeff was an adult when
he began offending, he still couldn't stop by
himself. He needed help.

Jeff also had a false "image." He acted like he
had a lot of self-confidence, but he didn't. In
treatment, he admitted that underneath his
image, he felt like "a phony." With help and
support he was able to find the real self that
was underneath his "image."

Can you see that in many ways Jeff had to deal
with the same issues as you do?

Questions:

**What are some of the thinking errors Jeff
used in his past?**

Did Jeff betray his victims? How?

**What do you think Jeff felt like when he
got caught and his name was in the
newspapers and on TV? What do you
think his family felt like?**

**Do you think treatment has worked for
Jeff? What did he say that makes you
think that?**

Chapter 44:
Cal

Cal grew up in an orphanage. He was taught that his body was bad. He doesn't remember being hugged or kissed by anyone until he was in his teens. Cal started offending when he was 23; now he's in his 40s. He has five victims. He has been in treatment for four years.

Sometimes you went long periods of time without offending. Why was that?

I didn't go out and create opportunities, but when they were there, I took them. Mostly I abused younger women I would meet on my job.

How did you feel when you first went into treatment?

When I listened to what other guys did, I went, "I don't belong with these guys." Some had molested young boys and I thought, "they are really perverted." I didn't even think about the fact that I had molested my own son when he was a year and a half.

How long did it take for you to participate in treatment?

It took me a year and a half before I realized I belonged in group. That I am one of "those people."

Before you started treatment, were you in touch with your feelings?

I didn't feel emotions, and I didn't

think other people did, either. I didn't believe that people cried because they had a reason to. I thought they were putting on an act. It wasn't until I was in group that I started recognizing that I do have feelings. Then I started admitting that other people's feelings were real, too.

What was the hardest part of treatment for you?

Telling myself that I was as bad as everybody else in group. My self-image was that "I'm a Nice Guy." To admit I was something different – a sex offender – was really hard.

Inside, did you think you were a nice guy?

Never. I didn't feel good about myself. I felt inferior to everybody else. I did things for other people, but only to make myself look good. Now, looking good in other people's eyes is not the most important thing. Feeling good about myself is.

When did treatment really start working for you?

When I finally told the truth and said all the nitty gritty things I really didn't want to say. I felt 40 pounds lighter. Nobody jumped on me, either. Instead, the group was supportive.

What is the most valuable thing you learned in treatment?

Being honest. Before, I did a lot of lying by omission. Now I don't hide anything.

Did other people notice when you got more honest?

It seemed like people had more respect for me. I started looking people in the eye. I disagreed with people sometimes. Before, I'd never do that.

How has your self-image changed?

I always used to feel I was lower than everyone else. Now, I don't look down on people, but I don't look up and think that person's better than me. I'm at an even level.

Have you suffered any losses because of being an offender?

I really like kids. I love to make them laugh. I always wanted to be an adult that kids could laugh with, because I never had that.

Now, I can't have any contact with minors. I really miss that. Even after my probation is up, I will not initiate contact. I don't want to put myself in a risky situation.

I can't have contact with my step-daughters, either. The daughter I did molest doesn't want anything to do with me.

Would your life have been different if you had had treatment earlier?

If I had gotten treatment earlier, it would have saved a lot of people a lot of grief and pain.

What advice would you give to teen offenders who are just going into treatment?

Do you really want to be a sex offender? Do you want your next 50 years to be good years or rotten ones? Are you willing to take two or three years out of your life now, to learn about yourself, change your life?

If you're not, you're going to be in the system the rest of your life. And no matter what you accomplish, your life will be a lie.

Cal learned a lot in his treatment. He learned how he had shut off his feelings. He learned that he didn't need to keep up his "Nice Guy" image. He learned he could be who he was, and get still get respect. He learned he didn't have to "look good" to please other people.

It took him a year and a half to admit that he is a sex offender. That's a long time. Offenders who go into treatment in their teens don't usually take that long. That's because denial hasn't become so much of a habit with them. Denial that goes on for a long time can become a way of life. It can take an adult much longer to cut through a pattern of denial.

Questions:

Why did Cal believe he didn't need to be in treatment at first? What is that called?

What happened when Cal got honest in his treatment? Why do you think that happened?

What do you think about Cal's "Mr. Nice Guy" image? Have you tried using that image? Have you seen someone else use it? Do you have a different image that you use?

What does it feel like when people respect you? When they don't?

Chapter 45:
Miguel

Miguel spent 4 1/2 years in out-patient sex offender treatment. He also has had big problems with drugs and alcohol. Today he says, "I'm in awe sometimes. I just can't believe the difference in where I was, and where I am today."

What was the hardest thing for you to "get" in your treatment?

The biggest thing was I didn't understand that when I offended, I was really hurting somebody. I didn't know people suffered trauma from being abused. I didn't know it dragged on them for the rest of their lives.

My dad had abused me when I was younger, so I thought abusing was OK behavior – that it was just what people do.

How old were you when you first offended?

As a teenager, I molested boys who were 4, 5 maybe 10 years younger than me. I did it to get my needs met. I came out about being gay when I was 18. I didn't molest again until I hit 29.

What made you re-offend?

After getting my fifth drinking and driving ticket I went to live in a small town. There was no gay scene there at all. I moved in with a woman, and ended up molesting her 6-year-old son.

What was the most important thing you learned in treatment?

The most important thing was learning how much offending hurts people. The second thing was how to connect with people. I didn't know how. Part of that was because my mother abandoned my sister and I when I was 5. And the next year my dad molested me.

In group, I learned how to make friends. I didn't know how before group. I thought friends were people you drank and did drugs with. I didn't know that friends shared their pasts, their hurts and feelings, as well as good times.

When you were offending, were you cut off from your feelings?

Oh, yeah. The drugs and alcohol did that. And the whole thing about having my sexuality be accepted. I used to try to hide my sexuality from people, but I don't do that anymore. I don't shove it in people's faces, but it's not my problem if they can't handle it. It's their problem.

What was hardest part of treatment for you?

To accept that it's OK to make mistakes. I learned that part of being human is making mistakes, that I don't need to be perfect.

I also learned to take responsibility for myself. Before I got into treatment, there was no responsibility in my life. None, whatsoever. Nothing was ever my fault. I was a victim of the world. I blamed everything that happened on my job, or my relationship, my father, my mother, alcohol. I was never the responsible one.

Why has this treatment worked for you, when all the other drug or alcohol programs didn't?

The other programs didn't work because I didn't want them to. I wasn't ready to feel my feelings. And that's one of the major keys to treatment: you have to be willing to feel hurt, to feel vulnerable.

What deterrents help keep you from re-offending?

I've made some rules for myself: If I'm feeling uncomfortable with someone, it's OK for me to leave the situation. I don't have to be a doormat. When I start agreeing – when I don't really want to agree with something – that's a red flag for me.

It's also OK for me to say "No," and I don't owe anyone an explanation. "No" is just "No."

What can you tell young offenders about going through treatment succussfully and making it on the outs?

Admit what you've done, and take responsibility. You can't even get up to

home plate if you don't. I've seen guys minimize over and over. "Well, yeah, I had one victim" even if there were 12 more in the wings he isn't talking about. Another thing is you can't isolate. Isolation will kill you. Get a support group – friends, adults, teachers. I'm still in a lot of contact with the people I went through groups with.

Life is hard. Growing up is hard. You can't have everything the way you want it, when you want it. Things take time. You can have your dreams and goals, but they won't come true right away. You have to work at them, be patient.

Why do you think it's important for youthful offenders to get treatment early on in their lives?

Number one, so they're not creating more victims. That's the first thing.

Number two, you're going to keep on acting out sexually, I thought molesting was just a phase I went through when I was a teenager. Then, at 29, 30 yrs old, I did it again. If you don't deal with it now, it'll happen again. Either you deal with it, or the system will. Or someone will put a gun to your head.

Miguel was a very unhappy person, but he didn't want to face it. He had "stuffed" a lot of sad and angry feelings from his past – about his abuse, his sexual identity, not having a family. He stayed numb by drinking and doing drugs. After a while, he didn't think other people had feelings. That allowed him to sexually abuse younger kids. He also didn't want to admit he was a sex offender. For a long time, he believed his of-fending behavior would just disappear. Did it?

Questions:

What role do you think drugs and alcohol played in Miguel's offending?

Do you think gay people are more likely to offend than people who aren't gay? Why?

What does it mean to "accept yourself"?

Before he went through treatment, Miguel did a lot of blaming. Do you blame others for your behavior? Who do you blame the most often?

Miguel has learned how to make real friends. What is a real friend? How can friends help you keep from re-offending?

Have you ever thought your sex offending behavior would just "go away" on its own? Have you ever thought you could stop abusing others all on your own? Do you still feel that way?

Section 12. Female Offenders Speak Out

Chapter 46: Alexis and Stace

If you're a guy, you may have been surprised to learn that females can be offenders. If you're a girl, you might have thought you were the only one. Knowing that other girls have offended may have come as a kind of relief. The girls in this section started offending in their early teens and have both been through treatment.

Many of the issues girls face in treatment are just the same as the ones boys do, but some are different. Maybe you can spot some of the differences.

Alexis

What did you feel like when you first went into treatment?

I was really scared, because I was going to be the only girl in the group. I didn't talk very much, I just listened. I was really nervous.

Do you think some treatment issues are different for girls than for boys?

In the group, they've done all the same things as me. I don't think I'm different that way. The same things are hard – talking about our offenses, having to be really honest, learning about our feelings.

But one thing I learned is that girls offend because they want to be closer to someone. Boy offenders don't talk about wanting to feel close or get someone's attention. Usually they want the power.

Whenever I was offending my little sister (we're only two years apart) I would always want her to look at me, to have eye contact. With my brother it would be the same thing. If they turned away from me, I would always make them look back at me. I wanted them to pay attention to what I was doing.

That made me feel connected to them. It made me feel that I had the power, too. That I was in control of the situation.

Any other way that being in group with boys is different for a girl?

Sometimes I feel that the boys are not as truthful – about what I say in group – as they would be if I was a guy. I think they don't want to hurt my feelings, but I want them to be truthful. Then I'd know what they really feel about me.

Yvonne

Did you go through group treatment?

No. I was in individual counseling. I never went to group.

Do you think girls who offend have different things to deal with than guys who offend?

Yeah, because most of the time it's the role of the man to offend. Now they're discovering females can do it, too. If they could, they should have a separate group for just females. Females would rather talk to females, and males would rather talk to males.

Do you think some of the issues females have to deal with are different?

You're looking at the whole thing from a different point of view, that females "shouldn't do this type of thing." Females aren't perfect. We deal with things differently than men do. Men think of women as being a mother, never hurting a child. It's really hard to discover you can do that.

What would you tell other young female offenders?

Don't keep hiding, because it comes back and haunts you. It haunts you everyday. They'll get you sooner or later. You better hope it's sooner than later. You don't want it to be later. You don't want to get charged as an adult.

Get help. It'll be hard. But you'll understand yourself a lot better. You'll understand who you are, the person that's hiding. You'll understand why that person wants out. And you won't be so starved for control anymore.

According to Alexis and Yvonne, girls do face some different issues in their treatment. Alexis says she offended her younger brother as a way of feeling connected to him. The need to feel "connected" is something male sex abusers don't talk about.

It was very hard for Yvonne to accept that she was a sex offender. In this society, people don't believe females can sexually abuse others, but she knew she had. She felt very isolated and ashamed of herself. (You should know that Yvonne ended treatment feeling good about herself. She was determined not to re-offend.)

Questions:

Were you surprised when you first learned that females can be sex offenders? Why, or why not?

Do you think that females have to deal with different issues in their treatment than males do?

Was wanting to "connect" with someone an important part of your offending behavior?

What treatment issues are the same for males and females?

If you found out a girl in your school was in sex offender treatment, how would that change how you viewed her?

Section 13.
Two Final Questions and Some Answers

"You have to find the true you ... Treatment gives you the chance to get your self back, so you can have your life back."

We asked these offenders who've been "telling it like it is" to answer two last questions we thought might help you. The first was: "What advice would you give kids who are starting treatment?" You know them pretty well by now. See if anything they say is helpful to you.

MONTE *"In group, what you say is going to be very hard for you. But the people in the group are not going to laugh at your offenses, your victims, or at you. I've told several people, 'We laugh at your jokes, not at your offenses.' When you talk about your offenses, it's something we all take seriously.*

There's never a problem that you can't work through. When you try, others will want to help you."

JAY *"Accept treatment. It's all here and it's going to be hard. You're going to have your ups and downs. But if you get honest and start doing your program, you'll start getting healthy. If you resist, you only make it hard on yourself, and you won't get anywhere."*

STACE *"What you did was wrong. You did hurt another person. But don't burden yourselves all your life about it. Get your treatment. Do what you need to do to not do it again."*

ELI *"Express your feelings. Let people know how you feel. Then everything else will come easier."*

ADAM *"What you did was wrong. You gotta let treatment help you out. You can't change what you've done, but you can let treatment change you. If you use the treatment it'll make your life a lot better. You start looking at things from a whole different perspective."*

ALEXIS *"If there are any girls out there reading this, and they are offenders, my advice is to go ahead and tell everything. You can get help. Treatment is a lot better than going to jail. Sure, sometimes it's hard, but it's the only way you'll get better."*

YVONNE *"In treatment you have to fight for your own self-dignity, to find your self again. You have to find the true you – not the abusive you, but the you that was there before that, but hidden. Treatment gives you the chance to get your self back, so you can have your life back."*

Take a few minutes and write down what you would like treatment to do for you. What kind of person would you like to be a year from now? How would you like to change your life? What would you like to throw out? What would you like to bring in?

Keep this list. Whenever you are having a hard time in treatment, read it again. Remind yourself how you would like to change, and why. Remind yourself that treatment gives you the chance to be the best person you can be.

The second question we asked these offenders was: "**As a sex offender, you have contributed to the problem of sex abuse in this society. How are you going to contribute to its solution?**"

Have you thought of ways you could do something to help heal the harm you have caused? Or what you could do to stop child abuse? Maybe some of these answers will give you some hints.

DEL *"Talk to my children about it, and about what I did. Tell them how wrong it is. Tell people about the tools I've learned. Maybe someday I'll go to a sex offender treatment program, and tell them my story. Maybe that would help some offenders learn about themselves."*

MONTE *"I can help by letting people know that not all offenders are evil people. That many of us are people who have made mistakes and need help. Another way is by giving all that I can in my group, and supporting others in their treatment."*

JAY *"I know sex offenders, what their attitude is. I could probably sniff out a sex offender on the outs by their attitude or the way they act. If I meet someone and have a feeling there's abuse going on, I'll do something about it.*

You know, people make fun of us because we're on the sex offender cottage. I say to them, 'Have you had sex with a girl who's been drunk?' They go, 'Yeah.' I say, 'Right there, that's date rape.' One way or another, seems like everyone's offended someone, somehow. I intend to let people know that."

ELI *"If I find out about somebody being abused, I'll talk to them about it, if they want to. I'm already doing that. I'm also paying for my victims' counseling."*

BEN *"What I can do to help stop abuse is to help other offenders change. One way is to sit down and talk with other kids in my group if they're having a hard time.*

Another way I can help is by not re-offending. People should be more aware of sex offender behaviors. If I see someone else behaving the way I did, I'm going to watch them, and see what they're up to."

BARRY *"I can help by making society more aware of what offending behavior is. One way is by telling people they need to talk to younger kids, so kids can know when they are being offended.*

Coming here and successfully working through this program is another way to help stop abuse. Then people know you have the tools not to re-offend.

We're always going to be sex offenders; we're always going to have those kinds of thoughts. To have the tools to be able to deter yourself is really helpful. It's also helpful for society to know you've successfully made it through a sex offender program."

Healing happens in a circle. When you do something to help repair the harm you have caused by offending, it helps you heal, too. Have you thought about what you might do to make up for some of the pain you have caused by your offending behavior? Maybe it's too soon in your treatment to think about that. Maybe you already have some ideas. Or maybe you think you shouldn't have to do anything.

This is a good issue to talk to your counselor about, or to talk about in your group. See how many ideas you can come up with.

Questions:

Did you notice any thinking errors in the answers these offenders gave?

How have the offenders in this book helped you to learn more about yourself?

Do you have any advice to give to kids who are entering treatment? What is it?

Will you always see yourself as a sex offender? Why or why not?

How can you help our society deal with the problem of sexual abuse?

We've come to the end of a long trip. We hope you've learned a lot along the way. We hope this book has led you to ask a lot of questions. We hope your group and your counselor helped you find the answers.

Some parts of this book may not have meant much to you right away. As you get further along in treatment, read those parts again. As we've said before, as you go through treatment, you will change. You might find that different chapters will mean more to you when you read them a second time.

As you continue to do your treatment, remember that Monte, Del, Yvonne, Barry, Eric, Stace, Ben, Jay and all the rest of the offenders in this book are behind you. They are trying to change their lives, just like you are. They know it isn't easy. They know that sometimes you feel very alone with all you have to deal with. They want you to remember that you're not alone. They don't know your name, but they are rooting for you. They wish you success in your treatment, and in your new life.

Good Luck!

Appendix

Thinking errors

Here's a list of thinking errors for you to read over. Do any of them sound familiar to you? Have you ever used any of them?

Assuming – Thinking something is true when you have not checked to make sure.

Blaming – Pointing the finger at others instead of taking responsibility for something you've done.

Catastrophizing – Saying something is a lot worse than it really is. Example: When somebody doesn't like you, telling yourself, "I'm a zero. No one will ever like me." Or when you fail a test, telling yourself "I'm stupid. I'll never get this right."

Closed channels – Stopping listening, expressing your thoughts and/or participating, whether you're in a group or with someone else. This is often done if you are angry or if you are playing the victim.

Distracting – Getting off the subject or trying to make another person forget what they were talking to you about.

Excuse making – Making up reasons why you shouldn't be held responsible for your actions. Example: "I forgot." or "I wasn't sure what to do."

Image – Putting on a false front instead of being your real self. Telling stories or acting tough to try and impress people.

Lack of empathy – Thinking only about yourself and not noticing or caring about other people's feelings.

Lying – Saying something that isn't true.

Lying by omission – Leaving out important parts of what the person you are talking to wants to know about. For example, telling your mom or dad about how fun science was and leaving out that you got in a fight and had to go to the principal's office.

Minimizing – Making things seem smaller or less important than they really are. Example: "I only did it once."

My way/Power play – Trying to overpower other people by bullying or tricking them in order to get your way. Anger and image is often a part of power play.

Procrastinating – Putting things off. Procrastinators often say things like, "I forgot," or "I didn't have enough time."

Projecting – Taking your feelings and pretending that they're coming from the other person. Projecting lets you pretend that your victim was the one with sexual feelings and that he or she approached you, instead of the other way around.

Super optimism – Acting as if things will happen just because you want them to. Example: "I'm so smooth, I'll never get caught."

Vagueness – Deliberately not being clear so it's hard for someone else to understand what the truth really is.

Victim playing – having a "poor me" attitude. Trying to get people to feel sorry for you so you won't have to feel responsible for your actions.

Select Safer Society Publications

Back on Track: Boys Dealing with Sexual Abuse by Leslie Bailey Wright and Mindy Loiselle (1997). $14. A workbook for boys ages 10 and up. Foreword by David Calof.

Assessing Sexual Abuse: A Resource Guide for Practitioners edited by Robert Prentky and Stacey Bird Edmunds (1997). $20.

Impact: Working with Sexual Abusers edited by Stacey Bird Edmunds (1997). $15.

Supervision of the Sex Offender by Georgia Cumming and Maureen Buell (1997). $25. Practical manual for probation/parole officers, court and treatment personnel, police, families and others.

STOP! Just for Kids: For Kids with Sexual Touching Problems Adapted by Terri Allred and Gerald Burns from original writings of children in a treatment program (1997) $15.

Shining Through: Pulling It Together After Sexual Abuse (Second Edition) by Mindy Loiselle & Leslie Bailey Wright (1997). $14. A workbook for girls ages 10 and up. Revised edition includes sections on sexuality, self-esteem, and body image.

A Primer on the Complexities of Traumatic Memories of Childhood Sexual Abuse: A Psychobiological Approach by Fay Honey Knopp & Anna Rose Benson (1997) $25.

The Last Secret: Daughters Sexually Abused by Mothers by Bobbie Rosencrans (1997). $20.

37 to One: Living as an Integrated Multiple by Phoenix J. Hocking (1996). $12.

The Brother / Sister Hurt: Recognizing the Effects of Sibling Abuse by Vernon Wiehe, PhD (1996) $10.

Men & Anger: Understanding and Managing Your Anger for a Much Better Life by Murray Cullen & Rob Freeman-Longo. Revised and updated, new self-esteem chapter. (1996). $15.

When Children Abuse: Group Treatment Strategies for Children with Impulse Control Problems by Carolyn Cunningham and Kee MacFarlane. (1996). $28.

Adult Sex Offender Assessment Packet by Mark Carich & Donya Adkerson (1995). $8.

Empathy and Compassionate Action: Issues & Exercises: A Workbook for Clients in Treatment by Robert Freeman-Longo, Laren Bays, & Euan Bear (1996). Fourth workbook in a series of four for adult sex offenders. $12.

The Difficult Connection: The Therapeutic Relationship in Sex Offender Treatment by Geral T. Blanchard (1995). $10.

From Trauma to Understanding: A Guide for Parents of Children with Sexual Behavior Problems by William D. Pithers, Alison S. Gray, Carolyn Cunningham, & Sandy Lane (1993). $5.

Adolescent Sexual Offender Assessment Packet by Alison Stickrod Gray & Randy Wallace (1992). $8.

The Relapse Prevention Workbook for Youth in Treatment by Charlene Steen (1993). $15.

Pathways: A Guided Workbook for Youth Beginning Treatment by Timothy J. Kahn (Revised Edition 1997). $15.

Pathways Guide for Parents of Youth Beginning Treatment by Timothy J. Kahn (Revised Edition 1997). $8.

Man-to-Man, When Your Partner Says NO: Pressured Sex & Date Rape by Scott Allen Johnson (1992). $6.50.

When Your Wife Says No: Forced Sex in Marriage by Fay Honey Knopp (1994). $7.

Female Adolescent Sexual Abusers: An Exploratory Study of Mother-Daughter Dynamics with Implications for Treatment by Marcia T. Turner & Tracey N. Turner (1994). $18.

Who Am I & Why Am I in Treatment? A Guided Workbook for Clients in Evaluation and Beginning Treatment by Robert Freeman-Longo & Laren Bays (1988; 8th printing, 1997). $12. First workbook in a series of four for adult sex offenders. Also available in Spanish.

Why Did I Do It Again? Understanding My Cycle of Problem Behaviors by Laren Bays & Robert Freeman-Longo (1989; 6th printing, 1995). Second in the series. $12.

How Can I Stop? Breaking My Deviant Cycle by Laren Bays, Robert Freeman-Longo, & Diane Hildebran (1990; 5th printing, 1995). Third in the series. $12.

Adults Molested As Children: A Survivor's Manual for Women & Men by Euan Bear with Peter Dimock (1988; 4th printing). $12.95.

Family Fallout: A Handbook for Families of Adult Sexual Abuse Survivors by Dorothy Beaulieu Landry, M.Ed. (1991). $12.95.

Embodying Healing: Integrating Bodywork and Psychotherapy in Recovery from Childhood Sexual Abuse by Robert J. Timms, PhD, and Patrick Connors, CMT. (1992). $15.00.

The Safer Society Press is part of The Safer Society Foundation, Inc., a 501(c)3 nonprofit agency dedicated to the prevention and treatment of sexual abuse. We publish additional books, audiocassetttes, and training videos related to sexual abuse prevention and treatment. For a catalog of our complete listings, please check the box on the order form (next page).

Order Form

Shipping Address:

Date:

☐ *Please send a catalog.*

Name and/or Agency
_____

Street Address
_____

City	State	Zip

Billing Address (if different from shipping address):

Address
_____

City	State	Zip

Daytime Phone (   )
_____

Purchase Order #
_____

Visa or MasterCard #   Exp. Date
_____

Signature
_____

Qty	Title	Unit Price	Total Cost

Make checks payable to:
SAFER SOCIETY PRESS
US FUNDS ONLY.

All prices subject to change without notice.
1- 9 items add $5 for shipping & handling.
10 or more, add 8% for shipping & handling.

Sub Total	
VT residents add sales tax	
Shipping	
TOTAL	

Mail to:
Safer Society Press
PO Box 340
Brandon, VT 057330340
(802) 2473132

Phone orders accepted with

Bulk order discounts available.
Rush Orders - add $10.00 and call
for actual shipping charges